CROSSING
THE SWELL

To Patricia

Thankyou for
your your
support

Fond Wishes

Paul Rees

CROSSING THE SWELL

AN ATLANTIC JOURNEY BY ROWBOAT

BY TORI HOLMES & PAUL GLEESON, WITH LIAM GORMAN

RMB
Victoria Vancouver Calgary

Rocky Mountain Books
#108 – 17665 66A Avenue
Surrey, BC v3s 2A7
www.rmbooks.com

Rocky Mountain Books
PO Box 468
Custer, WA
98240-0468

Library and Archives Canada Cataloguing in Publication

Holmes, Tori
    Crossing the swell : an Atlantic journey by rowboat / Tori Holmes, Paul Gleeson ; with Liam Gorman.

First published 2006 under title: Little lady, one man, big ocean, by
    Paul Gleeson and Tori Holmes with Liam Gorman.

ISBN 978-1-897522-53-0

    1. Gleeson, Paul, 1976 or 7—Travel—North Atlantic Ocean. 2. Holmes, Tori—Travel—North Atlantic Ocean. 3. Rowing—North Atlantic Ocean. 4. Transatlantic voyages. I. Gleeson, Paul, 1976 or 7 II. Gorman, Liam III. Gleeson, Paul, 1976 or 7. Little lady, one man, big ocean. IV. Title.

GV791.H64 2009   797.12'30922   C2009-903722-X

Front cover photo: Wave Wash by David Freund

Printed in Canada

Rocky Mountain Books acknowledges the financial support for its publishing program from the Government of Canada through the Book Publishing Industry Development Program (BPIDP), Canada Council for the Arts, and the province of British Columbia through the British Columbia Arts Council and the Book Publishing Tax Credit.

This book has been produced on 100% post-consumer recycled paper, processed chlorine free and printed with vegetable-based dyes.

This book is dedicated to the memory of Lynda Cantrell.

CONTENTS

ACKNOWLEDGEMENTS

To all our sponsors, especially Appleton Capital Management, we would like to say a big thank you. This trip would not have happened without your generous support. Thanks also to Fyffes, Irish Life, Vivas Health, Cornmarket Group Financial Services, Devon Town Council, Westwood Health & Fitness Clubs, Dun Laoghaire Marina, Artizan Design Studio, Nisku Rotary Club, Osborne Recruitment and also *The Irish Times* for chronicling our trip.

Tori

I would like to thank my family for all their support: to my father, Tom, for giving me the mental strength to row an ocean, and my mother, Fran, for always giving me emotional stability and being my rock. To my brother, Clayton: thank you for always believing in me even when it did not make sense, and to my Auntie Peg for inspiring me to push limits and acknowledge the world. To Jeannine MacAlpine: thank you for always being there for me at the drop of a hat. To our roommates and dear friends Daragh Brehon and Miriam Walsh: thank you for getting us to the start line, and to all our other friends along the way who took a chance on us: thank you. To Eamonn and Peter Kavanagh: thank you for believing in us. Most people would have dismissed the idea of two non-rowers wanting to row across an ocean, but you didn't, and I thank you for this. To Liam, thank you for all your help, patience and supreme guidance on this book. It has been an absolute pleasure working with you. In RMB we found enthusiastic allies. My biggest thanks go to Paul for sharing this experience with me, for pushing me to my limits and believing I could row across this ocean. Most of all I thank Paul for the unconditional love he has given me.

Paul

Although Tori and I were the ones out on the ocean, an adventure like this doesn't happen without the help and support of many people. First, to Eamonn and Peter Kavanagh, thank you just doesn't seem enough, but I'll say it anyway. Thank you very much for all your guidance, wisdom and support, and for having the faith to lend us your boat, *Christina*, to use in the race. We would not have got to the starting line, let alone completed the crossing, without your help.

To my parents, Bert and Lourdes, thank you from the bottom of my heart for putting up with me and supporting me on this adventure. I know over the years I have caused you many a sleepless night, and probably a few grey hairs, but your support kept me going in my darkest hours. To my sister, Audrey, thank you for standing behind me on this; you are the most selfless and supportive person I know and I am proud to have you as my sister.

I would like to thank all my friends who helped us out in so many ways leading up to the row, especially Donagh Nolan, whose straight-talking and organizational skills were needed at crucial times, and to Daragh Brehon and Miriam Walsh, who were there for us throughout our preparations. By virtue of the fact that we live together, I suppose you had no choice, but thank you for being so understanding and supportive. And finally and most important, thank you, Tori: your strength, courage and determination were immense and inspirational throughout the row, and I feel so fortunate to have shared so many wonderful adventures and experiences with such a special person.

Liam ··

This book, a little like the Atlantic crossing that inspired it, sometimes seemed an unlikely project. A series of *Irish Times* articles were small first steps. But could a working relationship built up through often patchy satellite phone calls thrive as the three of us chronicled Paul and Tori's adventures in book form? Like the row, the dream took wing. And, like the row, the credit lies with the two people whose story you are about to read. They are a remarkable couple: determined, inspirational and great fun.

Personally, I would like to thank my family for their support and patience. My children, Peter and Anna, are little bundles of joy who showed a surprising talent for quietness. Their mother, Suzanne, was calming and encouraging. She is the light of our lives.

Tori ··

In the past week we had been at the mercy of Mother Nature and discovered she has no mercy. I wrote in my diary on December 29, "How low can you go?" We had no water and then devastating amounts of water. And we came through.

We were two non-rowers who took on rowing the Atlantic; a student and a financial adviser who became adventurers. Could our relationship survive? Could we get across the Atlantic? Through these days the question was simpler: would we live or die?

Our water-maker started to fail on us. It went from producing 16 litres of water in an hour to none. Not long after Christmas, our satellite phone had run out of credit, and the phone company's head office was closed for the holidays. So we could not ring the water-maker technician to sort it out. The filters looked a little brown. We convinced ourselves this was the problem and took the water-maker apart to get at the filters, which were screwed into a plastic container. All we would have to do is open the container, replace the filters, and that would be the end of our problems.

Unfortunately, nothing in this row was ever that straightforward. The bloody plastic container would not open. We spent about 30 minutes trying to open the container before I remembered a rhyme my dad had taught me as a child when I would help him build his motorcycles: "Tighty righty, lefty loosey." We had been turning the container as hard as we possibly could . . . in the wrong direction. I sat there trying to open the container with all my might, fearing I would thirst to death if we could not open it. After a month and a half at sea, my hands were like those of an 80-year-old – they just would not work. It was strange to be surrounded by water and be so thirsty, to have a fear we might die of thirst. I remember wishing the water-maker was broken with a problem out of our control because if we were to die due to being too weak to open this bloody container it would feel like we had been subjected to the most evil torture.

This led to one of our major meltdowns. Dehydration really started to affect our coping skills. We lay on the deck of our small boat trapped in the ocean and just sobbed. At that moment I was the tiny child who had been denied what she most wanted. I really believed my world was coming to an end.

We had fresh water on board but it was ballast – and, under the rules of the race, once we broke into it we would be penalized. We decided to continue rowing, limiting ourselves to five litres of water a day. This was truly torturous. We rowed for two hours in the blistering heat, allowing ourselves less than one-eighth of a litre (we're talking sips here) per shift. All I wanted to do was grab the whole bottle and chug it down. The inside of my mouth was like a desert. With every sip I could feel it rush through my body. For a few seconds I would have renewed strength, not just in the body but, most important, in the mind. After those few seconds of bliss, I came crashing down, already waiting till the hour passed so that I could have another sip.

Because we had so little water, we also had to sacrifice meals. We just ate biscuits and energy bars. We could have cooked using seawater, but you can get quite ill from that, so we decided against it, at least in the short term.

Our spirits started to suffer. Emotionally, mentally and physically we were slowly breaking down from the inside out. We had no water to drink, or for sanitation and washing. Just when we thought it could not get any worse, I developed a kidney infection as a result of not drinking enough water to flush the bacteria out of my system. How do you get rid of a kidney infection? Same way as you prevent it – drink water. Since that was not possible, I took antibiotics for three days and the infection eventually cleared.

Three painful days into our drought the phone rang. It was the best sound I had ever heard in my life – we had contact with the outside world! It was Eamonn Kavanagh, our mentor back in Ireland. He told us all the teams were finding the race difficult. Teams were struggling with their steering lines and many of the water-makers had broken down. We were not alone. We did not wish misfortune on any other team, but we found comfort in knowing they were struggling, too, and pushing through it. It meant we could as well. The sound

Rules of the Race Regarding Water Ballast

Water ballast is required to be securely stored on the centre line of the boat to aid the self-righting capabilities of the boat. Mandatory water ballast also acts as a reserve drinking water supply should there be a problem with the boat's water-maker.

At the start of the race, water ballast containers are sealed by the race scrutineering officers, and on finishing, the containers are checked again to see if any of the seals have been broken. In a case where water ballast has been used the relevant penalties are allocated on a sliding scale as follows:

First 5 litres of water ballast used: 1-hour time penalty.

Second 5 litres of water ballast used: additional 6-hour penalty.

Third 5 litres of water ballast used: additional 12-hour penalty.

More than 15 litres of water ballast used: drop 1 place in the race.

More than 60 litres of water ballast used: drop 2 places in the race.

During the Atlantic Rowing Race 2005, the first three boats to cross the race finish line all had to drink their mandatory water ballast after experiencing serious problems with their water-makers. The penalties incurred by these crews were as follows:

Boat No. 24–*All Relative*: used 120 litres of water ballast, which incurred a penalty of dropping two places in the race rankings.

Boat No. 4–*Atlantic 4*: used 60 litres of water ballast, which incurred a penalty of dropping one place in the race rankings.

Boat No. 30–*Spirit of EDF Energy*: used 60 litres of water ballast, which incurred a penalty of dropping one place in the race rankings.

When mandatory water ballast is used for drinking water in this manner, crews are required to replace the empty ballast containers with seawater to maintain a constant level of the required ballast, so that safety in the event of a boat capsize is not compromised.

(Thanks to Woodvale Events, organizers of 2005–2006 race)

of Eamonn's voice was comforting. To hear his support for us meant a lot, as we had spent the last year trying to prove to him we could handle anything; we could take on an ocean. In our eyes Eamonn was the master of the ocean. His advice completely refocused us – now we were ready to fight back.

Eamonn called the support boat and told them of our situation. They arranged for Scott, the water-maker technician, to call us. He told us the filter was not the problem. Because the swell was so big, the skin fitting on the side of the boat was not able to stay submerged in the water as the waves rocked the boat and so air was getting into the system. Scott told us we would have to bleed the air out of the water-maker for two days. We did this and got the water-maker to work, but we only had a temporary solution. The air was out, but how could we prevent it getting back into the system? We certainly could not control the swell.

During the two days we spent trying to fix the water-maker, we confirmed with the support boat that we would not be disqualified if we drank some of our water ballast. There was a time penalty, which started with one hour for the first five litres we drank and an additional six hours for the second, all the way up to dropping two places in the race for drinking 60 litres or more. At this stage we knew we wouldn't win the race and the bottom line was that we needed water to live. We opened only two five-litre bottles and drank them over two days. We learned later that some of the leading boats had opened bottle after bottle.

We wanted to make our water-maker work. It is amazing how creative you can become in an extreme situation. We decided to rig up a service hose and bypass the sea strainer that sucked the water from the side of the boat. We would manually bail the water into jugs for an hour each day. It was very time-consuming and cost us days in the race, but we were like lotto winners. We had a second chance. "That which doesn't kill you makes you stronger" was our motto.

As it turned out, we needed this confirmation of our inner strength. The weather was ready to throw more challenges our way.

When our long wait for winds and following seas finally was at an end, we wondered if we had wished too hard. I looked up and it was as though a wall was rushing toward me. The swell was enormous and unpredictable. Everywhere you looked there were waves breaking,

The Water-maker

The water-maker works by extracting the salt out of seawater, making it drinkable. It takes 99 per cent of the salt out of the water. To make ten litres of fresh water the water-maker takes in approximately 100 litres of seawater, spits 90 litres back out and retains ten litres of filtered water.

The seawater is sucked in through the inlet hole and passes through a sea strainer, which is to prevent seaweed and any other loose debris from entering the system. The water is then passed through a charcoal filter, which removes some salt and impurities. Then the water is pumped through a membrane that removes the remainder of the salt. It will only allow water molecules to pass through it; salt molecules are too large.

In *Christina*, the fresh water supply was stored in a tank positioned in one of the centre hatches on the boat.

curling over each other. The ocean had thrown aside its friendly, welcoming demeanour. The water turned a surly grey, and the atmosphere became chilling. Sometimes the waves reminded me of two bulls ramming: they would charge at one another, each determined to master the other; eventually one would break and allow the other to collapse over it, spraying foam everywhere as if claiming its territory. As I clenched tightly to the oars that bounced up and down and from side to side, it felt like I was performing in a rodeo, not rowing a boat.

And then the horse threw me. I saw a wave rush toward me and I knew this one was different, dangerous. The boat climbed like a car speeding up a hill in San Francisco. Suddenly the top of the wave turned a light-greyish colour, as though the water had thinned out. I had no idea what was going to happen next. I saw a rush of water coming directly for me, like an animal jumping right at my face. It launched me from my seat, threw me down and bounced me against the side of the boat, the gunwale, nearly washing me overboard. I could see the boat coming over on top of me, the oars bursting from their gates as the stainless steel rods, which were there to hold them, bent back with the immense pressure of the water.

The boat bounced back like a basketball. The oars had actually prevented the boat from completely capsizing. I was absolutely terrified and in a slight state of shock. We had just come within inches of capsizing – who knows, maybe within inches of losing our lives. I was also completely pissed off, as the two oars we had lost were the only oars with my Canadian flags on them. I knew I would have to give in and row with the Irish oars. Paul rushed out of the cabin looking terrified. He had woken up as the wave hit the boat, to the sound of my scream. He saw my feet in the air amidst the white foam and was then thrown sideways.

When Paul got to me I was very shaken up. I had whacked my ribs very hard, and I could barely breathe or move. We tried to call my doctor on the satellite phone but could not get through. Within hours my ribs started to swell and bruise. My nerves were shredded for a while. We had to mend one of the gates that held the oars. I helped Paul put on the harness so that he could lean over the side safely, but I couldn't control my temper. I would freak out any time I looked in the toolbox as everything in it had rusted. They were supposed to be stainless steel – how could they rust? I was convinced someone had ripped us off.

Huge waves broke over Paul's face as he took on the job with a vise grip in either hand. I thought he was going to drown without actually entering the water. There was pure frustration in his eyes as he dropped a bolt into the ocean. Then the vise grips went in. A wave smashed him across the side of the boat, and he landed straight on his back on the metal rails that hold the seats. His face showed his agony – he would recover well, but he had aggravated a really serious injury, a vertebra, broken when he was nineteen. He got back up and stared down the ocean as though it was personal, as if the ocean had purposely taken him down and was out to get him. He would not let it go – he attached the bolt and saved the day. Then there was a look of satisfaction, as though he was thinking, "I'm McGyver right now!"

I was in pain, and I didn't know what to do. We couldn't reach my Mom, so I called my best friend, Jeannine, a nursing student. I had a huge medical kit but was not sure what medication to use. I held myself together for about five minutes and then completely broke down. I could not figure out which drug was the painkiller. The phone line was terrible and I could barely hear Jen as she rifled through her nursing books to check the medication. I felt helpless.

I started to panic. Every time I took a breath, a rush of pain would shoot up my esophagus. I started to feel lightness in my head. The more anxious I became, the more pain I felt. In this moment I was four years old again; all I wanted was my mom. I knew if I could just get through to hear the calming sound of her voice, the inner confidence she brings to my life would calm me down.

Paul stopped rowing and came into the cabin knowing this moment was more important than making two miles this hour. I had reached a point beyond reason. Paul knew he would have to be the rock, and over the next hour he repeatedly called the doctor until he made contact. It turned out I had a really bad case of acid reflux. Rummaging through the medical kit, I discovered we had everything known to man except something to deal with reflux.

The clever doctor suggested eating toothpaste. It's filled with calcium and neutralizes acid – yuck! If you have ever eaten toothpaste, you know it's horrible. He also identified the strong painkiller to dull the pain in my ribs so that I could continue rowing. I had to really dig deep to push myself on, as every time a wave hit a shard of pain would shoot up my ribs. I looked to my dad for strength, as I often have throughout my life.

He had texted me for the first time. "Push through the pain, face the fear to Valhalla and back, you're a Viking!" How did he know I needed these words? Later, I found out that Dad texted me because of a dream. He said all he could see was my head in water, my hair up in the air like I was falling and pure terror on my face. The dream repeated itself. He woke in the middle of the night, sweat running down his face. He was thousands of miles away, in a mine in the Northwest Territories of Canada, yet his intuition was still strong. He knew I was in trouble. He was probably feeling my anxiety. There he was, in spirit, to my rescue, as always. So I took the quote and recited those words every minute of every shift for the next two weeks, putting myself almost in a trance-like zone. In the end, I did what I had to do.

Paul

Dear God, could this get any harder? The night was moonless, and I couldn't see the breaking swell as it sneaked up on me. But I could hear it, and that was worse. It was like a roaring train coming toward me; I saw only darkness and could not brace myself for the breaking wave. Out of nowhere – boom! It floored me – threw me back off my seat and belted my back and shoulders off the deck. I spat out a mouthful of saltwater, grimaced at the ocean and shouted, "Fuck you, is that all you've got?" I was up for a fight tonight, and I bloody well got it.

My moods were swinging as never before. I am a fairly upbeat sort of guy, not prone to being down or depressed. But there were days on this trip that pushed me beyond anything I had ever had to cope with. Sometimes I just broke down. On day 46 I wrote in my diary:

> Very tired and drained today, ocean is very rough, it seems like this gets harder and harder every single day. Pup [my pet name for Tori] also feeling quite low today. Read Duggan's letter [Philip Duggan, a close friend] to pick us up; very thoughtful letter with lots of quotes from famous people about persistence and keeping going when things get tough. It did help, but then it seems the ocean senses you are feeling better and goes even more mental at you. I swear she's a bloody mind-reader. Ate a Mars bar out of our grab bag today around 3 pm as a pick-me-up . . . I read Dad's letter again to lift me, broke down in tears at the end of it . . . we're pushing ourselves beyond our limits at the moment, cannot do much more.

This probably was my lowest point on the trip. This is the letter Dad wrote to me:

> Dear Paul,
>
> This letter will hopefully find you on day 7 of your trip. It is so difficult for me to imagine the journey you have begun and what stretches out ahead of Tori and yourself. I hope when you are reading this that you are satisfied with the progress made so far. I have no idea how

far that might be but so long as you consider it reasonable progress that's good enough for me.

I have never written a letter to be put aside and taken out to read at an agreed timetable but then you have never set out to row the Atlantic before! It's a bit like putting some words in a time capsule. I suppose in truth I have never had to write too many letters to you at any time but despite that, I do think that our level of communication is special and I hope that will always be so.

You are both amazing people – quite rare in fact and that makes me very proud and I'm sure that goes for Tori's folks. You must have enormous strength of character to get you even to this point. Most people would be so afraid of even agreeing to undertake the voyage, never mind having the strength and determination to put so much work into the project for so long before even getting to the starting line. The amount of determination you have both displayed has been fantastic and in another context has been inspirational to others. That inspiration will undoubtedly continue and become even greater with each passing day and the realisation of this dream for both of you will be something very, very special indeed. The inspiration which will follow the successful completion of this voyage will be enormous and I cannot begin to try and calculate what that will mean.

Youth (even at 29!) is such a strong driving force and you are both using your abilities to the limit. Nobody can deny you that. There may have been many light moments of banter, ball hopping etc since you announced this incredible effort but even though I am writing this several weeks ahead of your departure, I can already see reality dawn on quite a few. Their own (and my own!) lack of courage [and] mental and moral strength are severely tested in merely observing what you two are about.

As you know so well, Paul, this is not a project which your parents could muster enthusiasm for. What self-respecting parent would wish to see their children put so much challenge and danger into their lives by choice? It is an instinctive thing for parents to want to help their children throughout all their lives to achieve goals but usually the issue of personal safety is not a factor. Consequently our overriding emotion has been focused on that issue, as I am sure you have easily understood.

The start line has now been passed, however, and although our instincts remain constant, we are, as we always have been, your most ardent supporters and always will be. I believe in your great determination, your courage as well as the strength you possess both mentally and physically. To have even contemplated doing what you are doing and to have followed through this project to this point took a single-minded (and somewhat selfish!) attitude to make it happen. Believe it or not, I am aware of that attitude. When the voyage is over, you will retain that determination and it will bring you both great success in life and it is that above all that I look forward to see come to fruition.

I love you more than you can ever know and probably if the truth be written, more than I would allow myself to demonstrate. Why that is, God only knows. It is surely a gender issue. If you have any doubts in your mind because of the vast horizon which opens out ahead of you, forget them! I have seen your determination at work in the past. I have no doubts because I have nothing but the highest opinion of your abilities. I know you will give this project your all, as will Tori, who showed such great fortitude and sheer guts whilst on your last mission together in Australia. Please do so safely and do not step outside of any limits that might jeopardise either of your safety. Please think of this at all times.

During the week before you read this, I will reach a milestone that I neither care to remember nor have any reason to speak about. However, it might be appropriate to share it with you since you will hardly meet anyone today who will be interested. On Wednesday, November

29th, I will have been working for 40 years with only the usual holiday breaks each year. So in the context of what you two young people are about, my life probably seems very dull. I don't think so myself! I have a collection of my own achievements, the most important of which is just being your dad.

Both of you have so much to offer the world and so much you can achieve.

God speed you beautiful people and keep you safe.

Dad xox
(Remember where that came from! – she is also rooting for you!)

Paul ···

Good times. We were driving out of Queenstown in New Zealand, three good friends having the time of our lives. Ray Niland chucked a book at me, *It's Not about the Bike*, the autobiography of cyclist Lance Armstrong. "Have a read of this. Absolutely savage read," he said. Bevan Cantrell had been stuck in it as well, and claimed it was the most inspiring book he had ever read. It gripped me too. About halfway through, I had an overwhelming urge to take on a big challenge myself. It didn't take long to come up with one – why not cycle across Australia when I got there!

I am a man who can be inspired by what I read. A year earlier, back home in Limerick, I read *An Unsung Hero*, about the heroic Irish Antarctic explorer Tom Crean. After finishing it, I felt the need to put myself through some sort of physical test, so I hopped on my bike and told my mother I was off to Dublin. Ten hours and 200 kilometres (124 miles) later I arrived in the capital. Despite the pain in my rear and the feeling that the saddle was about to come out my mouth, I felt a great sense of achievement and quiet satisfaction at my little adventure. In hindsight, maybe this planted a seed.

Like many other Irish twentysomethings, Ray, Bevan and I had saved up enough money to take a year out and go travelling abroad. This trip down under was our adventure of a lifetime, but unknown to me, the adventure was about to take on a whole new dimension.

After finishing Lance Armstrong's book, I felt an amazing sense of purpose; that I had just stumbled upon my calling, so to speak. My mind was constantly racing with ideas for the trip: What type of bike would I need? Could I do it on my own? Where would I start from? When would I be ready to go? I was buzzing inside. A fire had been lit, and I felt like a five-year-old looking forward to Christmas. Through the rest of our time in New Zealand, in between bungee jumps and sky dives, I was in internet cafés, researching my transcontinental cycle.

By Christmas 2002 I was living and working in Melbourne. I had started playing rugby with a local club and was enjoying my time in one of the best cities in the world. My parents and my only sibling, Audrey, were coming out to Australia for the holidays, and by now I had decided that I was definitely going to cycle coast to coast. I would start from Perth on the west coast with the aim of reaching Sydney six weeks later.

About a week before Christmas we were driving along the Great Ocean Road, a spectacular trip from Melbourne to Adelaide. In the middle of nowhere we saw a lone cyclist struggling into the strong headwind, his face a vivid picture of pain. His bike was heavily laden with saddlebags, which suggested to me that he was on a long-distance trip – perhaps he was cycling across Australia. Dad turned to me and said, "Where is that knucklehead going?" I turned toward the window. "Who knows where he's going?" I ventured, as nonchalantly as possible. I had planned to tell them about my planned adventure later that night, but this exchange warned me that they might not be thrilled with my plans.

That evening we had a quiet drink in the bar. I had a sip of my beer, took a deep breath and announced that I was going to cycle 5,000 kilometres across Australia. I waited nervously for the reaction. Audrey's reaction was typical of her character and the way she is toward me: curious, a little worried but almost immediately supportive. She is the most selfless person I know. Mam took a sip of her drink and said, "Ah, Paul, don't be daft." Dad realized immediately, I think, that my proposal was not an empty comment – his face said, "Oh no, he's serious."

Understandably, they were all a little concerned, and over the coming months, long after they had returned to Ireland, Mam and Dad attempted to talk me out of it and questioned my sanity. Why on earth would I want to undertake such a thing? In fairness, when they realized I meant what I said, they did support the idea, albeit in a slightly worried fashion.

The day after St Patrick's Day I bought my bike: a Mongoose Randonneur, a touring bike. The man in the shop thought it a bit odd that somebody who was not a cyclist was embarking on such a trip, but at this stage I was well used to people's reactions and I was 100 per cent focused. I really didn't care what people thought; I was going to do it.

There was a lot of preparation, and I learned very early about the need to have enough food to fuel the body properly. This lesson was given to me one evening while on a training cycle when I found myself 50 kilometres from my house, starving, thirsty and with no money to buy any supplies. It took me two hours to make it back to my house and every second of this was spent thinking about food and water. Then there was the equipment preparation; I knew nothing about the more technical aspects of repairing bicycles, things like changing gear and brake cables or replacing links in chains. I'm sure any experienced cyclist might not consider issues like these to be "technical," but to me they were. So with this in mind, I sat in while a bicycle mechanic serviced the bike, to learn how to fix everything that could go wrong. My training trips rarely exceeded 150 kilometres, however, simply because I didn't have the time – I was playing first-team rugby with the Melbourne Unicorns and we were top of the state league, so much of my training time was spent on the rugby field and not on the road. About a month before the start of the cycle, I broke two ribs in my last game for the club. I could have come back for more but I figured I might break something else and wouldn't be able to do the cycle. I was sad to leave the club – I had really enjoyed my time there and made some great friends.

I decided to give purpose to my cycling adventure and raise money for charity. I chose World Vision, a third-world development organization, and set a target of raising €250,000. My fundraising plan was simple: as I travelled across Australia I would sign up as many people as possible to sponsor a child. By encouraging people to contribute regularly instead of just giving a one-off donation, I would be able to raise more money. When I examined my route, however, it dawned on me I would not be able to spend much time fundraising, as I would be spending anywhere from six to fourteen hours a day on the bike. I needed somebody to come with me in a fundraising capacity, and I needed a car for that person.

Renting a car would be far too expensive. I tried a few car companies to see if they would donate one for the trip. No takers. I managed to get some companies in Melbourne to give sponsorship of a$3,000 (about c$2,700 at the time) toward a second-hand vehicle, and I bought a beautiful 21-year-old Mitsubishi Sigma that I reckoned would just about get across the continent. However, time was running out. There was less than a month to go, and I still didn't have anybody to come with me. Most of my friends were not in a position to take off for six weeks. I figured the only person in a position to do it would be a backpacker.

I printed up posters with the promise of free travel across Australia, the adventure of a lifetime and the chance to do a good turn for charity. Then I cycled around Melbourne putting up the posters in hostels. Surely they would appeal to somebody?

Tori

I was working in Sydney and living with a group of English lads. We returned home one evening to find we had been robbed blind. This was our cue to pack up what remained and head for the fruit-picking trail to try and sort out our finances. We drove to Melbourne in a broken-down camper van. The plan was to sample the good life for a few days and then head north in the van. I could feel an itch in my shoes, and I knew I needed to find an adventure soon. Going through the motions was just not enough. I did not know what I was looking for, but it had to inspire me. After all, I went travelling to challenge myself, not to sit in a camper van eight hours a day and watch my life go by.

I went into every hostel in Melbourne scanning the noticeboards for an original opportunity. The four English lads were eager to make tracks up north and wanted to leave that afternoon. On our way to the van I passed a little hostel off the beaten track. I hesitated, but despite the pressure to hurry up, I went in. Immediately this ad jumped off the tiny noticeboard at me. It said, "See Australia for free! Drive a support car for an Irish cyclist from Perth to Sydney and raise money for charity!" I could not believe it. It was as though this notice had been written for me. I was perfect for it. I had no money, so free travel was perfect, and the charity angle was inspirational. I ran to the van and told the boys I was going to do this. They did not want to wait around for Paul to get back to me. So I told them to leave without me. I think I truly began believing in myself at this particular point in my life. After all, self-belief was all I had. If Paul did not choose me, I was up shit creek without a paddle – stuck in Melbourne knowing no one and with no money.

Luckily for me, Paul returned my call, and we arranged to meet up outside the McDonald's in St Kilda. I knew I probably only had one shot at this, with the crucial free travel, and it played heavily on my mind. The pressure was on. I knew there would be loads of backpackers lined up for an opportunity like this.

As I waited I saw a young man hanging around. He was the only one around so I figured it must be Paul. My heart sank; this had to be a scam. The guy was a gangly youth and had big baggy shorts on, a skateboard he could barely stand on and a fag hanging very unattractively out of his mouth. What had I got myself into? Then I heard a polite voice from behind me: "Excuse me, are you Tori? Sorry I am late." Thank God! I turned around and was so relieved to see that Paul was a normal and at least athletic-looking guy. I wanted to hug him, but I thought that might be a little strong for a first meeting.

He took me to a little café nearby where we would discuss our future. Little did we know at the time it would turn out to be such a long future together. I felt immediately comfortable in Paul's presence: our conversation was natural right from our first words. He ordered a latte; I ordered a cappuccino. I had to order the cappuccino even though I am a latte girl, because I wanted Paul to know I was an independent woman, that I could handle the task in hand. That seems really silly when I look back at it, but it stands out in my mind as a memory. I think my independence and strength did come across. I gave the hardest sales pitch I have ever given to make sure I got the job. I told Paul my nickname was "slick Vic" (a name my father had given me during one of my first jobs, as a used car saleswoman). I set out to show I could sell ice to the Eskimos. I promised to have every sponsorship card Paul put in front of me sold. I think Paul thought I fancied him as I sat across the table and batted my little innocent eyelids. I made sure he had a good look at my little puppy-dog face. How could he refuse that? I thought it was no harm to try every angle. At the time, I was so focused on just getting the job that I was not really paying attention to the chemistry in the air. And I did get the job.

We would not acknowledge our partnership as anything more than a business affair until well into the cycle.

Paul

Tori made an impression on me immediately, with probably the firmest female handshake I had ever had. I was instantly taken with her spark and her sense of adventure. She was a very pretty young woman, but, probably for the first time in my life, I chose to ignore a woman's appearance and concentrate on her personality. After all, I would have happily done this trip on my own if I weren't trying to raise money for a charity. The only reason I wanted somebody to come with me was for fundraising purposes, so I was more focused on making sure I had the right person in that regard than I was looking to meet a girl.

As we sat drinking coffee and chatting about our fundraising ideas, I did notice that she was gorgeous: she had one of the prettiest faces I had ever seen. But the beauty of this young woman sitting opposite me was not my main focus. We got on really well and enjoyed each other's company. I was looking forward to our adventure together. Little did I realize what lay ahead for both of us!

On July 14, Tori and I pulled out of Melbourne, with the bike on a car rack, en route to Perth. We had spent a month making final preparations, but after driving the 700 kilometres to Adelaide, it suddenly dawned on me that this was a big country and that the cycle across it was going to be a long, hard slog.

But even the drive had its moments. We pulled into a small town called Crystalbrook, population approximately 200, for a toilet break. We walked into a small pub where a dozen or so locals stopped and looked us up and down. We felt like we were in a scene from *Deliverance*. However, a few beers later we were all the best of friends – we stayed there that night with hotel owners Adrian and Julie Lewis and left the next morning feeling a little green around the gills but having met some great people who gave us a super reception when we returned, me on my bicycle and Tori driving.

Next day, when we were literally halfway across Australia, our car, now christened "Bobo," broke down. We had blown the head gasket and were stuck on the side of the road in the middle of nowhere and with no phone reception. Out of nowhere an Indiana Jones–type character appeared and towed us to Kyancutta, the nearest village. There, the local mechanic, a great guy called Gadget, patched up Bobo. We got the part in from Adelaide that night, and by the end of the next day we were on our way. Again, we had met some fantastic people, and we stayed with Gadget and his wife, Susie, when we returned to Kyancutta on the cycle.

We finally made it to Perth, and after a quick dip in the freezing waters of the Indian Ocean, Tori and I set off on our 5000-kilometre Australian adventure. There were to be some miserable days ahead, and twice I would be knocked down. But my new friend, Tori, stayed by my side.

The first few days went well, but day 4 became the most painful day of my life up to that point. I had been having trouble with the new cleats on the bicycle, and my left knee was hurting. I was on the road at 7 a.m. but was in agony within minutes. I pulled into a town hospital and got knee supports, but they proved useless. Within an hour or so, both my knees were killing me. Every time I turned the pedal I got a sharp pain in both kneecaps. I had 150 kilometres to go to any civilization, so I didn't really have a choice; I had to keep going. The cycle that day was 235 kilometres. This should have taken me ten hours, but instead I was on the bike for 13½ hours.

And things got worse. The night was pitch black and I had about 10 kilometres to go, to a town called Kalgoorlie where we would be staying for the night. There were lights on the bike and I had a reflective vest, but I was watching for kangaroos jumping out at me and not feeling safe. Sure enough, a car came from behind and belted me. The driver was doing about 100 km/h and didn't see me. His side mirror smashed into my elbow, and I veered into the ditch. The guy came back and began falling over himself apologizing. I told him not to worry, I was fine. His hands were trembling, and he seemed a nervous wreck – when he hit me he thought he had killed me. When I think about it, he was probably only about a foot or so from killing me. I used his guilt for a good cause, and got him to sponsor a child.

We made it to Adelaide after a month. The knee injury cost us over ten days in mandatory rest time, as I could not walk for a few days afterward. Farther along the road, in some awful, rainy conditions, it would recur with a vengeance, leaving me cycling into Canberra on one leg.

A month later, on Wednesday, September 24, we were on the outskirts of Sydney. We would finally make it to the finish line at Bondi

Beach that day. World Vision said there would be television cameras. It was going to be a good day.

It was also going to be a very painful one. I was on the Princess Highway, only 10 kilometres from the finish, when I heard the screeching of brakes. A car smashed into me from behind and sent me flying over the handlebars. I landed hard on my left side, broke a bone in my left hand and couldn't really feel my arm and shoulder. But I didn't think this was too bad. An ambulance and a policeman arrived on the scene. "Where have you come from?" asked the policeman. "Perth," I said, casually. He looked at me a little funny and gave me a breathalyzer test.

I would cycle to the end – but not on the bike I had been using, as its back wheel was completely crushed. It was quite important that I get to Bondi for 11 a.m., as World Vision had told me the news crews were awaiting my arrival. I rang Kim, the PR person from the charity, and told her what had happened. I suggested that I run the last 10 kilometres, but Kim said it would probably be better if I arrived on a bike (after all, this was a cycling trip). So she organized a rental and dropped it over to me by 10:30 a.m. I got on board and did the 10 kilometres. After two months on the road, after many mishaps and laughs, Tori and I had finally arrived at Bondi Beach.

We had made no real plans for after the cycle. We were just enjoying the moment and our adventure. But even at this stage, I was taken with Tori's determination and free spirit. I wrote in my diary on that last day of the trip: "I don't want her to get a big head or anything but Tori is a very special and talented individual who I think we will all hear more about in the years to come."

We had become great friends by that point – and then, a bit more than friends.

Tori

I had slowly become intrigued by this man. He was so different, nothing like a guy I would normally go for. He was such a bloke, a man's man, a rugby player. He's a sports jock, I thought. Only as I got to know him did I start to perceive the many layers beneath his surface. There was a connection, a feeling we already knew each other, as if we had been friends for years. I trusted him almost immediately – bizarre, I told myself, as this man was a mere stranger.

Travelling across Australia, I noticed Paul's caring nature. All his amazing personality traits were fighting the voice in my head that was saying, "Keep it clean; keep it professional." I was quite young and had never given any one guy the time of day. I definitely had never thought about any of them this much. By the time we reached Perth by car, I had fallen for Paul. But it would not be until the end of the cycle that we would both openly express our feelings and move forward as a couple.

Paul ···

After the elation of completing the cycle across Australia, Tori and I spent a month together travelling up the east coast of the continent. I realized I liked her a lot. Was it love? I was not sure. I had never been in love before, but I knew the feelings I had now were new to me. We made our way up to a small town called Port Douglas, a short drive north of Cairns. Our time together was drawing to an end. It was October 2003; I was leaving Australia for Nepal, South Africa and South America, and Tori was staying in Australia for another four or five months.

On our last night we went out for dinner. As a backpacker in a hot country, you do not have that much in the way of fancy clothes or a huge amount of money, but we dressed up in our best gear and went out to a fancy restaurant for dinner to say goodbye.

Tori ··

This was probably the first time I had ever wondered if I was in love. No one had ever been able to keep my attention long enough for me to even contemplate love. I pulled back, as I felt I was too young for love and was uncomfortable with my lack of control over my own emotions. After all, this was not part of my plan. The time I spent with Paul was only supposed to be a moment in time. At this point, I was ready for Paul to leave. We decided that we would not wait for each other. We would go on living our lives, and if in half a year we still crossed each other's minds from time to time, we would deal with it then. Neither of us wanted to hold the other – or ourselves – back.

Paul ···

Tori drove me to the airport the next day. After I checked in my bags, we waited together until my flight was called. Tori disappeared once or twice to the bathroom, returning each time with her eyes that little bit more red. I didn't comment on it. I knew she would not want me to recognize that she was crying.

As we sat waiting for my flight to be called, I remember feeling sort of nervous and sad to say goodbye. We embraced each other one last time; I turned away and boarded the plane. I had this knot in my stomach, and as I found my seat and sat down, I wondered if I would ever see her again. We had made a genuine connection and had shared a very special experience together, but it was time for us to go our separate ways. Perhaps this would be a case of right person, wrong time!

I headed for the Himalayas; Nepal was somewhere I had always wanted to visit. I spent a month there, high up in the majestic scenery of this unique kingdom. It is a magical place but torn by strife between the king and Maoist rebels.

I travelled on and spent months in South Africa and South America. I still wondered about Tori and what might happen between us, so I decided to take a chance and head for Canada. Tori had returned home in February 2003 and was living and working in Vancouver. Toward the end of March, I boarded a plane in San Juan, Costa Rica, bound for that Canadian city. We had spoken once or twice on the phone since having parted in Australia, but we had not seen each other in five months.

I believe one should never have regrets in life. Better to do something now and see what happens than in the future regret not having taken the chance. This is the way I viewed things with Tori and me. Worst-case scenario: we would meet and one or both of us would not be interested. If that happened, I would enjoy a few weeks in Canada before returning home to Ireland. I had been away from home now for nearly two years and was looking forward to seeing all my family and friends again. But then I found myself wondering, "Well, what if Tori and I pick up from where we left off in Australia, what then?" I couldn't stay in Canada. I had to go back home because I had taken out a bank loan to finance part of my travels around the world, so I had no choice but to return and start working to pay it off. I decided not to think about it, just go for it and see what happened.

I was quite nervous getting off the plane. Would the spark still be there between us? Would either of us have changed? Would the physical attraction continue to have its spark? My appearance had changed quite a bit since Tori last saw me – my hair hadn't been cut in months, and I had a bushy beard.

In the end, it was a chance worth taking. We did pick up from where we left off, but this time the L word was used. And then we said our goodbyes again. I had to return to Ireland.

Tori

A few months after we met in Canada, I travelled to Ireland, initially for a reunion with a group of friends with whom I had lived and travelled in Australia. We met at the Red Hot Chili Peppers concert in Dublin, as our local bar had played their album during our entire time in Australia and we regarded their music as our own. My plans after that were vague. I was open to any opportunity. Through the next few weeks the spark relit between Paul and me. This is probably where our relationship would take a definite turn. I was willing to stay and work in Ireland for the summer to just see what might happen. I found myself unable to turn my back on Paul. After his travels he had this shine about him; he had come into himself. He had that sort of X factor I wanted to surround myself with, hoping it would rub off on me. He was my best friend, my biggest critic, my biggest fan.

I remained in Ireland over the summer. Paul and I had become as close as ever, but we faced a crossroads. I had not bonded with the way of life in Ireland. Visa requirements meant I was unable to work and thus limited my adventure. I felt unconnected. The first place you meet friends in a new location is usually at work, and being without work all my connections were through Paul. Being the independent person I am, I felt at a loss with myself for the first time. Where was the spark, the self-belief? I decided I would have to go back to Canada – either to stay or to get a visa so I could return and work in Ireland. As much as I was in love with Paul, I wasn't willing to change my whole life at the risk of being unhappy. I needed a reason to return to Ireland: something bigger than both of us, an opportunity I would not be presented with in Canada, a challenge. I wanted stimulation. The best way I knew to stimulate myself mentally, physically and spiritually was by embarking on an adventure. And, boy, what an adventure was about to present itself.

Paul ··

Nighttown, Limerick. Tori and I got into a taxi; my friend Shane was going somewhere else, so he waited for another. As he closed the door of our cab, he leaned in toward me: "Would you have any interest in rowing across the Atlantic?" His tone was of a man suggesting a game of golf. "Are you serious?" I asked. I suggested we talk about this after the weekend, during the sober light of day, and see if this was something we actually wanted to do. Too late. In my mind, I was already getting ready to compete.

Shane O'Neill is an old schoolmate who I had not seen for some time. We were both back home in Limerick and out on a Saturday night. My sister was leaving Ireland to go to work in Bahrain, and we were having a few beers in the Locke Bar by the river. Shane wanted to know about our cycling trip in Australia. He is big into physical challenges and is quite an accomplished long-distance runner. He also has a little mad streak that I like in a person; he thinks outside the box and isn't afraid to take risks.

Tori had not heard what he had said about the Atlantic row, but I was up for it straightaway. My brain told me, however, that it was too big just to say "yes" immediately. I needed to look into the proposal properly. As the taxi drove us home in the early hours of Sunday morning, I said nothing to Tori but my mind was racing with the idea of taking on the wild Atlantic in a rowing boat. I had never rowed a boat and had no ocean experience whatsoever. But, just like the cycle in Australia, the idea appealed to me enormously. I didn't know why or how I was going to do this, but I just felt that I could. I suppose since I had returned to Ireland after my two years abroad, I hadn't quite settled back and maybe subconsciously I was looking for another adventure.

On Monday I called Shane and we discussed the idea. How serious was he? He was deadly serious and told me that a company in England called Woodvale Events organized races across oceans and that the next one was across the Atlantic beginning in November 2005. As we finished speaking, Shane told me to check out their website for all the information. When I tried to log on I came across a bloody language institute site! I had typed in the website address incorrectly. When I finally found the correct address, the language was clear and uncomplicated. The race described seemed to me to be one of the toughest challenges in the world.

Once I started reading, I was hooked. The race would start at the Canary Islands and finish at the Caribbean island of Antigua. It was open to anybody between the ages of 18 and 65. The following line sealed it for me: "No rowing experience is required." This was all I needed to reassure myself that I could do it. If others had done this before, then why couldn't I?

I was lying in bed one evening and couldn't keep my secret any more. I turned to Tori and told her that in a little over a year I was going to row across the Atlantic Ocean. Her first reaction was along the lines of, "Oh my god, my boyfriend is nuts," but when I told her all about it and explained the history of the race, she said she wanted to do it as well. We had a team of three.

We contacted the race organizers who said they would allow us to race as a team of three but we would be in a category of our own, as all the other teams consisted of either two or four people or were solo rowers. Our hunt for a fourth rower began.

The choice of our fourth member was crucial. We discussed it at length and figured that the person had to be fit but above all his or her personality had to be right. We would have to get on with each other in a very confined space for up to three months. I knew that Tori and I were compatible. I was also close to certain that Shane would be a good fit. A few years had passed since we had been at school together, but I am a good judge of character and my gut feeling was that the three of us would make an excellent team.

Over the following weeks, I asked some of my friends who I thought might be interested. I made it very clear that if they wanted to join us this would have to become their life for the next year. If our team were not 100 per cent committed to preparing for the race, not only would we not cross the Atlantic but we wouldn't even get to the starting line. One or two people expressed an interest but said that given their overall circumstances (job, girlfriend, family) it just wasn't possible at the moment.

One of the first people I asked was one of my best friends, Bevan Cantrell. Bevan is one of the best rugby players I have ever played with: physically strong but above all else a tough individual with a big heart, the type of guy who would dig in when things got tough. He was very laid back, and I was certain the four of us would make a great team. Unfortunately, Bevan was not in a position to commit to the project.

I say unfortunately because that is how I viewed it at the time. But hindsight is a peculiar thing. In a letter that we opened at sea, Bevan wrote, "I'd love to have undertaken your challenge but my circumstances at the moment don't allow me ..." It seemed similar to the words used by others who had to decline our invitation, but Bevan's words turned out to be loaded with irony. On day 13 of the row, we got a call that reduced me to tears. Bevan's mother Lynda had passed away very suddenly. If Bevan had been out there with us he would not have been able to get home, would have missed his own mother's funeral and would have had to endure over two months at sea away from his family whilst trying to cope with the loss of his mother. It just doesn't bear thinking about.

The search for a fourth member went on. Donagh Nolan, or "Mole" as we have all called him since school, was living in England at the time. I knew him very well and thought he would be capable of doing the row. He was not an obvious choice, though. He played rugby in school and was a decent swimmer, but once he left school, sport no longer played a huge role in his life. Donagh enjoyed going out and having a good time, enjoyed a few beers. But this would all have to change if he wanted to join us on the Atlantic. He would need to get a basic level of fitness before even contemplating doing the row. However, he is a very determined guy, quite resilient and somebody who I knew would not give in when things got rough and dangerous on the ocean. I knew Donagh could get in shape for the Atlantic in time if he was up for it.

We told Donagh that if he decided to do it, he had to be in Ireland in the new year. To prepare for this properly, we felt we all needed to be in the same country, commit totally to the project and be fully aware of the dangers. I knew Donagh was the type of guy who would think of all these things anyway and would not take on such a challenge unless everything was right. In fairness to him, he immediately started to train with a rowing club in England and started doing his own research on the race.

Donagh is an engineer and works as a project manager. He looks for answers, deals in definites and takes a practical approach to things. All these are good qualities, but I didn't have all the answers to his questions. I could not give any guarantees and there was an awful lot of uncertainty. This was something we just had to go for and hope like hell we could pull it off. It was risky stuff. But in order to proceed with this, whoever was involved with us had to feel comfortable and willing to accept the level of risk.

Donagh took a month and then told us he was not going to do it. He was very interested but had had some back trouble in the past and within only a few weeks of training the pain had come back. Things might go wrong out on the Atlantic, and we might have to live with injuries and the like, but you had to start the race, at least, in one piece. Donagh had hoped that his back pain would ease as he got used to training hard again but it didn't, so he had to pass.

This was a real blow, as we were really hopeful Donagh would join us. Tori and I are optimists: if there is even an outside chance of something happening, in this case Donagh doing the row with us, then we tend to get our hopes up very quickly. I suppose having one's hopes dashed is the downside of eternal optimism.

On the face of it, our preparation was not going well. We did not have a full team; we had no boat, no money and no idea how to row. But for some reason we just knew we really wanted to do this and believed we could. It was as if we were children again and instead of looking at the stacks of reasons why we could not do it, we just focused on the fact that we wanted to do it. So why not?

We had a million things to do, and as we would find out over the coming months, we were very low on time. Many other teams would spend two years preparing for this race – and they were rowers. We needed to press on with learning how to row. We also needed to speak to somebody who had done this before. Only once had an Irish rowing boat made it across the Atlantic, and the men who rowed the boat were two brothers from Arklow: Eamonn and Peter Kavanagh. We decided to get in touch with them.

A Short History of Ocean Rowing

The first recorded Atlantic crossing in a rowing boat was achieved by Norwegians George Harbo and Gabriel Samuelsen in 1896. They rowed from New York to the Scilly Isles in 55 days and then on to Le Havre in France in a further five days.

This Herculean feat remained unmatched until September 3, 1966, when Chay Blyth and John Ridgway, in their boat *English Rose III*, landed on the Aran Islands on the west coast of Ireland, having rowed from Cape Cod in Massachusetts. They had spent 91 days at sea.

Fourteen other people rowed across various oceans between 1966 and 1982. Between 1896 and 1982, twelve ocean rows were completed. These are regarded by the Ocean Rowing Society as "historic rows," as they were done without water-makers, life rafts, satellite phones, Global Positioning Systems (GPSs) and Emergency Position Indicating Radio Beacons (EPIRBs).

The first transatlantic rowing race took place in 1997. Thirty teams set off from Los Gigantes in the Canary Islands on October 12 with the aim of reaching Port St. Charles, Barbados. Rob Hamill and Phil Stubbs's New Zealand team won the race aboard *Kiwi Challenge*. They rowed into Barbados after 41 days at sea.

The one Irish team in the race consisted of Eamonn and Peter Kavanagh, who finished fifth in their boat *Christina*. They completed the crossing in 58 days. This was the boat used by Paul Gleeson and Tori Holmes eight years later in the 2005 race.

Races were also held in 2001 and 2003. The 2005 race featured 26 boats, with four teams of four, 20 pairs teams and two solo rowers.

By the beginning of summer 2006, fewer than 300 people had been recorded as rowing an ocean. Tori Holmes (at 21 years of age) became the youngest woman ever to row across an ocean in 2006.

"Why did I do it? Because at the end of my days, I'm going to be lying in my bed looking at my toes, and I'm going to ask my toes questions like 'Have I really enjoyed life? Have I done everything I've wanted to do?' And if the answer is no, I'm going to be really pissed off." – Chay Blyth

(Thanks to Oceanrowing.com)

Tori ⋯⋯⋯⋯⋯⋯⋯⋯⋯⋯⋯⋯⋯⋯⋯⋯⋯⋯⋯⋯⋯⋯⋯⋯⋯⋯⋯⋯⋯⋯⋯⋯⋯

The tall, burly man asked only one question: "Can you row?" "No, never have before," I answered and then mumbled something about canoeing in school. "Well, get in the boat," said Eamonn Kavanagh.

Shane, Paul and I had come to the coastal rowing club in Arklow with bellies full of butterflies. We had tracked down Eamonn and his brother, Peter, the only Irishmen to have rowed the Atlantic. They had the reputation of having no time for time-wasters. You do what you're told or you piss off. Now we joined the real rowers in their beautiful, handcrafted wooden boat – a skiff – lifted the oars and found they were as heavy as tree trunks and as long as a car.

"Pick up your oars," Eamonn said. I struggled with the Arklow accent – in fact I wondered why this man from Wicklow spoke German. He looked at me as if I was daft; I smiled blankly and looked around for Paul. What on earth was this man saying? Paul pointed to the oars and we pulled, following the rest of the crew, trying to come across as not totally useless. Within five minutes we felt every muscle in our bodies burning.

Eamonn's instructions were short and to the point: "Pull on the port side [right-hand oar], Tori." He was speaking German again. And then he kept repeating it. I started to panic. Eventually Eamonn said, "Pull on the oar in your right hand." I wondered why he didn't say that in the first place, and I did what I was told. For now the spotlight was off me, but I sensed there were many more moments like this ahead.

A year later, a few days before we set off to row the Atlantic, Eamonn and Peter, Paul and I were out for dinner in La Gomera, the Canary Islands, and the brothers told us they thought I was a bit slow when they first met me. Any time they asked me something I would smile at them sweetly and answer a completely different question. We had a good laugh at it then.

But that first day of training was hard. The hands began to cramp, and drops of blood started oozing through our fingertips as the newly formed blisters burst on our baby skin, our "office hands." But we put on brave faces to try and gain the respect of these hardened sea dogs. As we headed back to the beach where we came ashore, Paul and I felt a total buzz. There was a look of seriousness on Shane's face; a glimpse of doubt, maybe. But Paul's imagination, like mine, was taking flight with the prospect of attempting such an intense and original task.

We realized that this was going to be very difficult, and maybe in a twisted way this was a spur for Paul and me. Eamonn Kavanagh doubted our enthusiasm and put us right back in the boat to push us even further. He was going to make this young couple understand the severity of what they were contemplating. It would not be a picnic, and Eamonn wanted us to know this straightaway. It would be like a prison camp, he said.

Eamonn and Peter live, eat and breathe the ocean and rowing. They are serious, hardened men, and I felt honoured to gain their respect. So up and down the Avoca River we went, struggling to keep in time with the other rowers. Every once in a while, the oar would fly back and nearly take my head off. It was like a scene from *The Matrix*, with an oar replacing a bullet – you either moved your body in anticipation or you got caught.

I got caught often. Once, Paul heard a faint grunt and turned around to see the soles of my feet swing above my shoulder – I was nearly airborne. I held on to the oar like a little pup dangling in the air. I quickly got back on the seat as the oar handle came around, hoping Eamonn hadn't caught a glimpse of my slip-up. Paul sniggered, and I snapped back. For a moment I was the panther – a personality assessment my mental coach would subsequently give me because panthers are quick to pounce.

The score was evened almost immediately, as the oar handle lifted Paul from his seat. The pup had a little snigger to herself. "You guys okay?" Eamonn yelled at us. "Grand, grand, yeah we're okay," Paul shouted back, trying to mask his obvious discomfort. I flashed back a fake smile. It would be in use a lot over the next year.

After this first session Eamonn took us up to the rowing club and pulled out some of the materials from their row in 1997. The first thing he showed us was a picture of the chafing. Eamonn and Peter rowed in normal shorts on a small wooden seat (ouch!). It was a picture of pain: a swollen backside covered with big open wounds. Such pain would become familiar in the not too distant future. I sensed doubt in Shane's eyes. Eamonn talked frankly of the dangers he and Peter had faced. He made absolutely nothing about the row look or sound appealing. We thought he was laying it on strong, using some scare tactics. But then, we hadn't yet rowed the Atlantic.

As Eamonn perused a chart, I asked to look at "the map." Eamonn looked up at me as though I had three heads. "It's not a map, it's a chart," he barked. He seemed shocked at our blatant lack of sea knowledge. What race exactly did we want to be in? The Woodvale transatlantic race, we replied confidently. Just short of a year away. His next words were very stern: "If you're serious, you've a lot to do. I'd be surprised if you're ready in a year. You can learn to row all right, but are you mentally tough enough and are you seaworthy enough?" Paul and I had absolutely nothing on which to base our self-belief, but for some reason we felt even more inspired to push on after Eamonn admonished us. This really was a challenge, an opportunity not to be missed.

Paul ···

Eamonn and Peter became our teachers, and Eamonn, in particular, our mentor. He was a hard taskmaster. One Sunday morning, Tori could not make it down and neither could Shane, so I went down to train in Arklow on my own. Eamonn took me aside for some extra training, something that had become the norm for Tori and me. One of the issues was basic seamanship: the practical skills and knowledge we would need to know to survive on the ocean. Usually over a cup of coffee or tea, Eamonn would go through these practicalities.

One Sunday, Eamonn spoke of a "bowline." "What's that?" I eagerly inquired. Eamonn nearly choked on his tea. "Are you telling me you don't know what a bowline is?" he asked, bristling. My heart raced. I had just done something wrong and was in trouble with my teacher at school. All of a sudden I was seven years old again (a feeling I would often experience around Eamonn over the next year or so).

A bowline is a type of knot that is frequently used to tie things up at sea. The beauty of it is that once it's tied correctly, the harder you pull, the tighter it gets. It was something we needed to know. Eamonn got up abruptly, went out to Peter's work shed and returned with a rope. "Right, look. This is how you tie a bowline," he said. I spent the next few hours tying bowlines to beat the band. When I mastered it, Eamonn instructed me to close my eyes and do it. There would be times in the Atlantic when we would have to do this in the dark. When this was mastered, he told me to close my eyes again and tie the knot around myself. Several hours later I emerged from the darkness of the kitchen proud of myself and my newly acquired skill.

As I drove back to Dublin that night I was like a child who had just learned a new card trick. I could not wait to show Tori my new-found skill. Tori spent the next week furiously practising her bowlines so that she could pull one over on Eamonn the following Sunday by casually tying this sacred knot upon request.

It seemed to be coming together. But our next challenge was much harder than anything we had faced in a boat.

Paul ···

The drive to Dublin should have been pleasant on this sunny day in October. But I was anxious. Shane said he would tell his family about the row over the weekend. The phone rang and my heart began to beat faster. Oh God, what would it be like when it came to telling my own family? There was no mistaking the resigned, sad and uncertain tone in Shane's voice. He told his family and they went mad. Then came the words I feared: "I don't know if I can do this now." Was our dream going to be shattered before it even had a chance to begin?

Right from the start, we always knew that one of hardest parts of this project would be breaking the news to those closest to us. There is no easy way to tell your parents that you want to put your life on the line and take on the might of the Atlantic Ocean in a 23-foot rowing boat. We all expected opposition.

The reaction of Shane's family was overwhelming. His fiancée, Kathy, who is now his wife, was put under pressure by the family to talk some sense into him. Shane was having second thoughts. I asked him then and there on the phone if he still wanted to do the row. He said he did but he wasn't sure how to handle the response he'd received to his plans for such a dangerous adventure.

Tori and I knew it was a selfish thing to do and that it would be difficult for our families. But we had to be single-minded. You do consider your family's feelings when planning to embark on adventures such as this, but at the end of the day each of us must live our own life and take responsibility for the decisions we make.

Shane opted out. In fairness he had a lot on his plate – he was getting married and planning to buy a house. And we still had not found a fourth member for our team. I do believe, though, that his family's reaction was a large factor in his decision. He was much more considerate of his family and friends than we were, and I'm sure they appreciated this. On hearing of Shane's parents' reaction, I told him that no matter how bad my family's reaction was, I still intended to do the row. But this would not be easy, as my family means the world to me and we are very close.

First up were Tori's parents, Fran and Tom. Back in March 2004, when I met Tori again in Canada after our five months apart, it had been meet-the-parents time. Tori's mother, Fran, welcomed me literally with open arms. She is an absolute gem: a lovely, warm woman. Tori's dad, Tom, is a 6-foot biker with nine tattoos. He's a heavy-duty mechanic who doesn't tolerate fools. Tori had told me many stories about how he treated her former boyfriends: basically he was one of those people you'd prefer to have on your good side.

I first met him when Tori and I were visiting some other family members just outside Vancouver. Tom arrived up the stairs. "So this is the Irish guy I've been hearing about," he said, his handshake firm. As we all chatted over the next hour or so, I was on my best behaviour. I'm sure he was sussing me out. At one point, as I talked to someone else, he called me. As I turned around he took my picture. "Now I have a photo of you in case you ever hurt my daughter. I'll hunt you down." I thought of a smart reply but decided to keep it to myself. I'm fairly sure he meant what he said. I get on very well with Tom now; he's a good guy, a real character. No more than I would if I had a daughter, he wanted to make sure I was good enough for his little piranha, and I respect that. I think he went easy on me, to be honest.

Tori

I feel very lucky to have had such a unique childhood. My parents are both very strong, independent characters. The values my parents practised and preached were: to be an individual, to challenge life, to shoot only for the stars. I am the person I am today because my parents nurtured my confidence and raised me and my brother, Clayton, according to our – very different – personalities.

When I was a small child I was so painfully shy, neighbours thought there was something wrong with me. But mother knows best. Mom stood by me, protecting my sensitive nature. Sure enough, one day I burst out of my shell, showed my true colours and never looked back.

I can probably credit my parents with my adventurous side. Among my fondest memories of my childhood is being tucked into the sidecar of a Harley Davidson for two months as we toured the west coast of

North America. We took in the largest biker rally in the world. Little did my parents know that these childhood adventures would be preparation for a much greater challenge later in my life.

I told my parents that when I finished school I intended to go to Bangladesh to visit my Aunt Peggy and hopefully find an organization to volunteer for. I don't think they believed me at the time, but at the ripe old age of 18, I packed my bags. Full of zest and ambition, I headed off to begin my journey in life. I would return home two years later with possibly more life experience than most 40-year-olds have.

When it came to our newest challenge, my parents' reaction was fairly calm and quite supportive. The general line was: "You're both nuts, but if that's what you want to do, then off with you."

Paul ....

Tori's mother, Fran, had maybe not grasped the full message when Tori first told her about the row. She called our house in Dublin one evening in early November. I was talking to her for a few minutes before she mentioned the crossing. "So you and Tor are planning to row across the Irish Sea," she said, enthusiastically. Oh dear. "It's actually the Atlantic Ocean," I replied awkwardly. "Hold on a second, Fran, I'll get Tori for you."

I didn't say a word to Tori, just casually told her that her mom was on the phone. As I gave the phone to Tori, I could hear Fran's screams of horror echoing from the handset: "The Atlantic . . . Paul, what do you mean? . . . Paul, are you still there?"

We visited Canada later in the year. Tom looked me in the eye. "Fair play to you, Paul, for having the balls to try this. But if anything happens to my daughter, I will kill you and hunt down your family."

Despite their worries, all in all, Tori's parents took the news fairly well. They had their concerns, but their attitude toward their children was along the lines of "You're an adult now, you have to make your own decisions, and we'll support whatever you want to do." I admire that, because I'm sure for most parents this is difficult, especially when confronted with the type of challenge Tori and I wanted to take on.

I was next up, and this was not going to be easy. I got on the phone to Bahrain and told my only sibling, my sister, Audrey, first.

She was surprised and had many questions, but Audrey is the most supportive and selfless person I know. She was worried about us but put these worries aside and offered her support. The preparations we had made, the skills and knowledge we built up to take on the Atlantic, were, I hoped, going to help me alleviate my parents' concerns – but poor Audrey couldn't see any of this at first hand, which is why I thought her support for us was so special. When she was home for holidays, I overheard her defending us to a cynic who was criticizing us. It seemed like such a loyal display on Audrey's part, sticking up for her little brother. Even though she probably wasn't exactly delighted that I would soon be heading off on such a dangerous adventure, there she was defending me with such passion to some cynical begrudger, and it made me feel very proud to have such a wonderful sister.

When I told my parents about the challenge, they were concerned and had a lot of questions. Why on earth would you want to row across the Atlantic? Beyond this, I think they were very worried that their son was moving from adventure to adventure and was not living in the real world. Would he spend years borrowing money from banks to do these crazy things and then spend the rest of his life trying to pay the money back? I think they were worried where my mind was. I know my parents just want me to be happy, but deep down I also realize that they would probably have preferred my dreams to be centred more on buying a house and settling down. I suppose having a child who courts danger must bring with it a mixture of worry and pride, possibly more of the former. It can't be easy.

By Christmas, my parents' worries had led to a slight rift between us. Tori and I were so busy preparing for the race that I wasn't able to see my folks as much as I would have liked. When I did, conversation centred on their trying to talk me out of the row.

At this stage, however, I was awash with all sorts of different emotions. My head told me that I was being selfish and should not pursue this, but my heart cried adventure. I felt like I was really living life; I just could not put this idea down. I was also becoming frustrated and slightly annoyed that my parents couldn't just accept my decision. After all, I was 29 years old and as Mam would often say, "You're big enough to look after yourself."

Although I could understand my parents' angst and really did not want to worry them, I had my own life to lead. No matter which decision was made, somebody would be pissed off. Ultimately, I decided that if I were to pull out of the race because I didn't want to upset my parents, this would be dishonest, both to myself and to what I believe in – that we get one life and we should live it to the max, making our own life choices. Audrey was a great help throughout this in that she spent many a long hour on the phone to Mam and Dad trying to reassure them that we actually knew what we were doing. I imagine that was not easy; she surely had her own doubts.

I am a very loyal person and my family means everything to me. It hurt me deeply to know that what I was doing was upsetting my parents and causing them so much worry. They had given me the best start in life anyone could have wished for. This was no way to repay them, but I just couldn't let go of this newly formed dream to take on the Atlantic Ocean in a small rowing boat. This was my life now.

Then another spanner was thrown in the works.

I was driving through town on the way back to the office after a meeting when my mother called. I did not want to talk to her about the row but it was very difficult not to mention it. It was the first thing that came into my head in the morning and the last thing I thought of at night. Even when I slept, I was constantly dreaming of this voyage. I was 100 per cent focused on this – Tori and I both were – and we had to be if we were going to even make the start line.

Mam asked me not to do the row. She told me it was causing her and my father an awful lot of worry and stress, and she was worried about the effects of this. Whether Mam was overworrying or not, I don't know, but she was being honest with me and I love her and respect her for that. She broke down in tears on the phone and my heart sank. I could not believe that my actions were doing this to the people I loved the most, the very people I would lay down my life for. After we finished our talk, I pulled the car over to the side of the road and burst into tears. I have never told anybody this or written of it until now. I felt so ashamed of myself. What if my actions led to something happening to the health of either of my parents? I would never be able to live with myself. It just wasn't fair on my folks. This was probably one of the most difficult times in my life; I genuinely did not know what to do.

At this point, I was on the verge of packing it all in. But I suppose if the row was going to be easy, anybody would do it. There were many elements to our preparations that weren't easy, but we were about to meet an amazing woman!

Paul ·····

Eight-thirty in the morning. The alarm screamed out the start of a new day. It felt like my eyes had just closed. It was a Sunday, and it was lashing rain outside.

I nudged Tori several times in an attempt to wake her from her deep sleep. Her eyes opened slowly, and we both peeled ourselves from our nice, warm bed. It had been a long week, and we were both tired as we pulled on our rowing shorts, eyes still not fully open. A quick bowl of porridge and we were out the door by 9 a.m.

While most of the country was enjoying a lie-in on this miserable November morning, Tori and I were making the hour's drive from Dublin to Arklow. This was our routine now. We rowed with Eamonn, Peter and the members of Arklow rowing club each Sunday morning, rain or shine. The club trained right through the winter and once it was safe we went out to sea to learn how to row. If Eamonn and Peter deemed it unsafe to venture out to sea then we stayed on the Avoca River. Safety was of paramount importance to these men. 'The first accident we have here will be our last,' said Eamonn. We learned very early on that the ocean – even the Irish Sea – is dangerous and safety can never be overemphasized.

We needed to keep coming down to row, first, because we had to learn, and second, because we had to prove to Eamonn and Peter that we were serious about wanting to row the Atlantic. Most Sundays Eamonn put us through our paces, and despite the fact that our hands often blistered and bled as we rowed, we were learning quickly how to deal with this discomfort. In fact once we woke up and got out on the water it was absolutely brilliant, no matter what the weather. If it was rough and wet, I imagined that we were on the Atlantic battling away with Mother Nature, as if we were in a Guinness commercial. When it was dry and sunny there was nowhere else I'd rather be. It was the one time during our hectic week when we could relax – all we had to think about were the oars. As we became more proficient rowers, the work even became quite soothing. Our Sundays with the Kavanaghs had quickly become my favourite part of the week.

Both Tori and I were becoming captivated by the draw of the open water. Peter Kavanagh had lovingly handcrafted the wooden skiffs we rowed in, *Dancer* and *Dasher*. These are sweep rowing boats, which means each person rows with one oar. There are four rowing positions in a skiff and the oars are quite long and heavy and need a bit of getting used to. We also trained in a pairs boat, which was quite light and allowed Tori and me to get used to rowing together. It enabled us to practise rowing with one oar in each hand, too, which is known as sculling; this is how we would row the Atlantic. Although we had yet to row in the type of boat we would use for the Atlantic race, the boats we were training in were an excellent place to start.

Most Sunday mornings after training we would go for a coffee with Eamonn in the town or back to Peter's house. Without our really appreciating it, an intensive learning process had begun. We would blitz Eamonn and Peter with all sorts of questions about the row, and they would educate us on aspects of life at sea and question us every week to see if we were learning what we needed to know. Some days I felt like a schoolchild again as Eamonn quizzed me on things I didn't know. But we would come away from these meetings inspired and fired up – and with a longer list of things to do.

On this Sunday, as we nestled into our coffee, I told Eamonn we needed to find a boat for the race. Eamonn and Peter still had their boat from the 1997 race, but I was shy of asking about it and so I had made some inquiries in England. "There's a boat here you can use if you like," Eamonn suggested, casually. "Are you serious?" I asked. "Yes." Could we buy it – or would they rent it to us? "There's no need, you can use it free of charge." Tori and I nearly choked on our coffee, our eyes and mouths wide with amazement.

Eamonn put his cup of coffee down and pointed a finger. His expression was grave. "You can use the boat on two conditions: first, you don't rename her – I don't mind you putting sponsors' logos on her or repainting her, but the name stays the same; second, you don't give up." This thought had never crossed our minds before. What did he mean? He told us that if things got too much for us and we packed it in out there, we could call the support boat. If we were picked up by it or by any other boat, we would have to burn the boat – his boat – as you cannot leave a floating craft in the ocean because it could be a danger to other seafarers. "Don't come back to Ireland if you burn my boat," Eamonn said. He was deadly serious. I knew I would rather take my chances with the Atlantic than face Eamonn and Peter after having burned their boat.

There was a considerable monetary value to the boat, but I know this was not the reason for the words of caution. Their boat was called *Christina* after their mother, who has since passed away. They had also built the boat themselves, so the brothers had an understandable sentimental attachment to it.

It is thought to be bad luck to rename a boat, and we told Eamonn that under no circumstances would we even consider renaming her. We also promised we would die out there before giving up. We meant it. We were so focused and intent on seeing this through that if we managed to get ourselves to the start line, it would be a cold day in hell before we would give up.

People often describe the performances of sportsmen or women as being such that it appeared as if their life depended on it. For us, our lives *would* depend on how we performed. Eamonn told us that although many people had died trying to row an ocean, nobody had ever died during this particular race, but that this would probably only be a matter of time. I agreed with him. This was serious stuff; the time to prove ourselves would soon come, or so we hoped.

Being put in charge of *Christina* was an enormous boost of confidence for us. The most experienced ocean rowers in Ireland were willing to lend us their pride and joy to take on the Atlantic again. Wow! Apart from saving us about c$30,000, which we would have had to pay to buy a boat, it meant so much that these legends thought that maybe we could do it. They didn't tell us this at the time, and we didn't ask any questions, but this is what we took away from this gesture. (Eamonn did tell me later that he did not think we would be ready in time.) We shook hands with Eamonn in the pub and that was it. Simple, old-school and straightforward; we made a promise we wouldn't give up and Eamonn took us at our word.

The timing was fortunate. Before we had found Eamonn, one of Ireland's best rowers, Gearóid Towey, had contacted him about the

Atlantic race and about using their boat. Gearóid, who represented Ireland in the Olympic Games of 2000 and 2004 and was a world champion in 2001, is virtually a full-time oarsman and also a very nice guy. He was to become even more famous when the boat he and partner Ciaran Lewis eventually used capsized, but this was all in the future. After making contact with Eamonn he left some time before speaking to him again, so Eamonn thought he had changed his mind about the race. However, about ten days after Eamonn had promised us the use of *Christina*, Gearóid rang him again to talk about the race. Although Gearóid wasn't 100 per cent certain at this point that he was entering, it speaks volumes for the type of men Eamonn and Peter are that they stayed true to their word in lending their boat to a couple of novices when one of the best rowers in the world might have used it.

Eamonn made it clear that we had work to do on *Christina*. She had been in the water only on and off since finishing the race in 1997. We would have to make a few fairly big structural changes to comply with race rules. We had equipment to buy. She would have to be inspected by a marine surveyor to make sure she was seaworthy. But for now, none of this mattered to us. We had just been given a boat. We now had a shot at getting to the start line. We were ecstatic as we drove back up to Dublin that evening.

Christina is 7.1 metres long (just over 23 feet) and 1.9 metres wide (6.2 feet). When fully loaded she weighs a little over 750 kilograms. She has two cabins: the aft cabin is at the stern, which is the back of the boat, and is the main space where we would sleep and store a lot of our food and equipment. She also has a smaller forward cabin at the bow, which is the front of the boat. This is where we would store other equipment, such as our sea anchor, life raft, toilet, tool kit, spare water-maker and much more.

There are also many below-deck storage compartments, where we would keep the first 55 days' worth of our food supply, our water-maker, cooking stove and gas, as well as our water ballast. The water ballast would consist of 150 litres of fresh water that would serve two purposes. First, it would act as a backup water supply for us in the event of our water-makers breaking down. We reckoned we could probably squeeze 30 days out of this supply if we had to. Second, it would self-right the boat in the event of our capsizing in the giant Atlantic swell. We would purchase our ballast in the Canary Islands in five-litre bottles, which would be sealed and stored in our centre hatches down the middle of the boat.

Although many would question the sanity of two people heading out into the Atlantic in a small rowing boat, these boats have all been specifically designed and built to cross an ocean. *Christina* had also been reinforced throughout with extra fibreglass by Eamonn and Peter when they built her. Peter has built quite a few boats, and anyone who knows him knows he builds boats to last.

Christina had crossed the Atlantic in 1997, and although we had quite a bit of work to do, mostly installing new equipment and making structural changes, she was in good condition and as solid as a rock. But we did not yet have the equipment or the funds to do what was required. We were struggling at this point: my relationship with my parents was very strained, and we had no money to buy the equipment we needed. But that was not all. We were now also running into a lot of negativity from unexpected quarters, so all in all things were not going well.

CHAPTER 8
Just Do It
NOVEMBER 2004

Paul ⸺

I walked into McSorley's pub in Ranelagh in Dublin. I knew there would be plenty of questions from friends, and I expected a bit of a grilling about my notion of rowing across an ocean. But I was really taken aback by the negativity. It was an ambitious challenge and nobody wants to see any harm come to a good friend, but instead of "Yeah, go for it, but be careful," it was more a case of "Don't be stupid, you can't do that, you're an idiot for even thinking that." One man, a friend's father, said, "When is that fella going to come into the real world?"

We did expect this sort of reaction from some people. After all, who were we to think we could row across an ocean? We couldn't row; we had no ocean experience, no boat, no money. But we both had something that is not tangible and cannot be shown to friends and family, something that neither money nor a boat will give you: self-belief. This and this alone would be the source of our strength and courage over the coming months. Still, I really had hoped for a more supportive initial response.

I soon began to thrive on negative reaction. Although it disappointed me that people were not as supportive as I would have hoped, the more negativity I encountered the more driven I became. I embraced it and maybe even subconsciously sought it out. Even at this early stage, failure was not an option. Tori and I were so determined to make the start line we would not accept anything less. But we had many hurdles to overcome. As fired up as we were, we needed a little bit of luck if we were to make the race start in November. Pro golfer Gary Player once said, "The harder I practise, the luckier I get." I am a firm believer in this. You can have all the talent or self-belief in the world, but if you don't work hard, you can forget it. We were working hard but we needed to keep working like dogs if we were to have any chance of making our dream a reality.

Around this time I was struck by the amount of begrudgery in Ireland. I know it's a generalization, but why do we insist on knocking people down if they think a bit outside the box or want to do something a little different? Is it insecurity? Perhaps we don't want them to succeed because it may reflect badly on us. At what point do so many people lose their ability to dream? When do they lose sight of their childhood ambitions?

By December we knew we had to make a big decision. Visa restrictions meant Tori was not able to work in Ireland and would have to return to Canada to apply for her working visa. She was struggling with life in Ireland, and I felt for her. Coming back to Dublin after two years abroad, I thought it was not the place it used to be. People seemed to be in an awful hurry and were often just downright rude and ignorant. Manners, it seemed, were becoming a thing of the past. Perhaps this is an unfair generalization, but it seemed true in Dublin society in particular.

Tori

I just felt trapped. I felt as though I was losing my character; that my spark and zest for life were being sucked out of me because of my situation in Dublin. I was there because of Paul, and that was just not enough for me. I couldn't work, which meant meeting friends outside of Paul's circle was virtually impossible. In my mind I was losing my independence. In fairness, Paul could see this and knew I was miserable.

Paul

Tori had been away from home for quite some time, and she was missing her family and friends. And I wanted her to go back. I did not want to see our relationship come to an end, but I wanted her to be happy and if that meant returning to Canada, then so be it.

I suspected that if Tori were willing to return home for a few months, see all her family and friends and then return to Ireland armed with her working visa, that this would make all the difference to her happiness. We both went to Canada after Christmas for a few weeks' holiday.

Immediately, I could see Tori finding her old self. The spark was returning and as each day passed in Canada, I could see her emerging – the pup was back!

Those January days in Vancouver were a turning point. Tori was happy at home and wasn't sure she wanted to return to Ireland. This was bittersweet news. Maybe it would be better for her to remain indefinitely. But what would this mean for our relationship? And what about the row?

When I need to clear my head, I like to run and think things over. One beautiful, snowy morning I put my long johns on under my shorts and went for a run through the suburbs. I decided that if Tori wanted to stay in Canada, I would row alone. I could not give up on this idea now. I also decided that if Tori did not want to come back to Ireland and do the row, we would have to break up.

Decision time. Tori said she would return to Ireland and give it another go. Since she was now armed with a working visa, I was certain she would enjoy it more and make her own friends through her work. As for the row, we still had much work to do, not only physical and mental training but also securing sponsors.

Back in Limerick over the Christmas holidays, the word had been out about the row. An old friend, Fergus Walsh, had told me over a few pints that he would sponsor us C$1,500 through his company, Appleton Capital Management. I could hardly believe it – we had our first sponsor. While we were in Canada, I called Fergus to see if he was serious about sponsoring us. He said that he was and that if we could put a logo on the boat and get some pictures with their T-shirts on, then there was C$4,000 in it for us. Consider it done, I replied. We also picked up two more sponsors in Canada. Tori's hometown council, Devon, agreed to sponsor us C$5,000, and the local Lions Club and Nisku Rotary Club said they would do something for us. We were on a roll! We thought we would have our sponsorship money raised in no time – little did we know!

The time had come to pay our registration fee of £300 to the race organizers, Woodvale Events. For us to participate in the race, we would have to pay a further £14,400 in race fees – and this was before the cost of a boat, equipment, food, shipping and much more. So, in the grand scheme of things, the registration fee was a small thing. But it was significant for Tori and me. Paying that fee was a sign of commitment.

I returned to Ireland in January knowing that Tori would come back in March. Those early months of 2005 were a hard time, a time of sacrifice. I knew that if I was to continue to pursue this dream, it was going to upset my family. Many of my friends thought I was mad.

Trying to organize everything that went with the row was starting to affect my job. And work was important to me; I had built up a good reputation and did not want this to change. Now I was having to push myself harder, sleep less, train more and work longer hours. Something would have to give, but I couldn't let it give if we were to make the start line. The candle wasn't just burning at both ends – the bloody thing was in flames and there was no putting it out.

There was also a social sacrifice to be made. Meeting friends and going out for a good time became a thing of the past. Tori and I just didn't have time. Over the coming months I would be asking friends to help us out with certain aspects of the row. I was conscious that I had become a man who only called his friends when he was looking for something. This was deeply discomfiting, but there was very little Tori or I could do about it.

The whole project involved hanging ourselves out there and taking a huge risk. If we managed to complete the row, people would say, "Wow, well done, you guys are great." If we failed to get to the starting line, people's attitudes would probably be more along the lines of, "You fools, what were you thinking of?" Even if we started the race and failed to complete it, we would be mocked by some, laughed at by others. And it was never going to be a secret endeavour – we had to seek as much publicity as possible to help us get sponsorship and to raise money for our chosen charity, Concern Worldwide, which provides emergency humanitarian and development aid with the goal of eradicating extreme poverty in developing countries.

Tori and I have never been ones to play it safe, and we decided that now was not the time to start. We were under pressure even at this early stage; we had so little time. There were many reasons why we should have called it a day. I am not an overly religious person, but I remember reading the following words on a mass leaflet: "If you wait till you're sure, you'll never do anything." There was so much uncertainty in the air, but we had made our decision. Now we just had to do it! But we needed sponsorship and we needed it fast!

CHAPTER 9
The Sponsorship Game
JANUARY–MARCH 2005

Paul ··

I was nervous as I walked into the reception of the Dublin Exchange Facility. As the elevator door opened on the first floor I brushed the palm of my right hand down my thigh to clean off the sweat. Fergus Walsh is a friend from my rugby days, but now I was also going to meet his brother, Dave, who is the managing director of Appleton Capital Management.

Months before, Fergus told me that Appleton would give us c$1,500 in sponsorship, then in a subsequent conversation raised it by $2,500. About 20 minutes into my conversation with Fergus in their offices, Dave Walsh came into the room. As I was speaking, Dave picked up our brochure and began browsing through the sponsorship packages available. I sensed that he was considering increasing their contribution, so I kept talking. I was ready to talk all day. Dave put down the brochure. "Would it help you if we gave you a cheque for c$15,000?" he asked. I nearly fell over as I muttered the words, "Yeah, definitely. Are you serious?" I felt like hugging him – actually, I think I did. Fergus, who was holding a cheque for c$4,000, looked at Dave. "Should I write a cheque for the balance?" he asked. "No, just tear that one up and write a new one for $15,000," Dave replied. It felt like a scene out of *Who Wants to be a Millionaire*. I punched the air with delight and then apologized for the display. I was absolutely overjoyed. The way Dave looked at it, by giving us a big contribution toward our costs, we would reach our sponsorship target earlier and so we could focus more on raising money for the charity.

Tori was still in Canada at the time, not due back until March, and I was finding the struggle to raise sponsorship hard on my own. But now, as I drove home, I was bubbling over with excitement. I called Tori when I got home to give her the good news. At this rate we would have our sponsorship money collected in no time.

Or so we thought . . .

Our plan was simple: get our proposals out to as many companies as possible and we would surely get enough positive responses to raise the money we needed. In total this project was going to cost us in excess of c$120,000. We learned quickly that it was not enough to send out sponsorship proposals randomly. We needed to put some thought into who we sent the brochures to. We had to consider how sponsoring us could benefit a particular company.

Many of the large companies in Ireland have sponsorship budgets and even sponsorship managers who decide how this money is to be spent. I learned a very valuable lesson early on when I contacted Allied Irish Bank. I spoke to their sponsorship manager at the time, Jim Kelly, who declined to back us and said they were focusing their sponsorship efforts on teams with grassroots emphasis – ones that reached into communities all over Ireland. Fair enough, I thought. He was very helpful and gave me some constructive criticism, advising me to think more about the type of companies we approached before we approached them.

We took his advice and tried to come up with a genuine link between us and each potential sponsor and tailor our approach to them accordingly. As time wore on, our links became more and more creative. This was enormously time-consuming. We regularly stayed up until three and four in the morning researching companies and writing up sponsorship proposals.

We discovered the truth of the old saying "It's not what you know but who you know." This is what sponsorship was all about for us. Often the most difficult thing was making sure our proposal got to the right person – the decision-maker. Getting past the secretary or personal assistant was often the hardest part of the game.

We also had to chance our arm. If companies actually knew how little we had and how much we had to do, most would run a mile. Most of them did anyway. One day I rang a company to whom we had sent a sponsorship package. I told them that such was the interest in the row we were "closing off" our sponsorship packages that month; if they wanted to get involved, now was the time. This was, of course, arm-chancing at its finest and I received a polite "no." At least I got an answer; that was one more ticked off the list.

We tried everything we could to raise our profile and encountered some great people. I heard a radio advertisement for the first outdoor adventure show in the Royal Dublin Society (RDS) in Dublin and met the organizer of the show, Victor Dunne, in a coffee shop in Blackrock. He is a likeable guy, full of life and energy. He asked me what our budget was, and I said zero. He laughed. He asked again, and again I reassured him that this was the budget. We eventually agreed on a very fair price for the boat to appear at the show on a stand. It took a lot of hard work to get the boat out of the water – with the help of a friend of Eamonn Kavanagh's who had a tractor – and I cleaned it up in Peter Kavanagh's back garden. I had to pay to have it transported to the show, and though we did get a minor sponsor out of it, this involved a good six months of badgering, persistence and follow-up phone calls.

Our next challenge was to find somewhere we could train properly for the next nine months. We needed a well-equipped gym near where we lived. Westwood Health & Fitness Club was about five minutes' walk from our house and I put together a sponsorship proposal for them and met the manager. Andy Hughes is a rock climber and a huge outdoor enthusiast. He is a fantastic guy and seemed to be genuinely taken by our plans to challenge an ocean in a rowing boat. We were given free use of the health club. We now had an excellent place to do our gym work.

Getting sponsorship is hard when you are unknown. Raising our profile was a time-consuming exercise. We didn't have the money to engage a PR firm so we phoned, faxed and e-mailed radio and television stations and newspapers. We were very surprised at the response. Many places simply were not interested, or told us to come back closer to the time. We decided that if companies knew they would get guaranteed television coverage, this would help our sponsorship drive. If we survived the trip across the Atlantic and could get a documentary made, it would be worthy of some airtime on Irish television. But the production companies we talked to said they did not have enough time to do it, and we did not have enough money to have it made independently. There were only so many hours in the day, so we had to focus on getting the practical things in place for the row.

Friday, March 11, was a good day; I had a meeting with Roddy Murphy, one of the directors of Cornmarket Group Financial Services, the company I worked for. He agreed to sponsor us to the tune of $4,000. We also discussed other companies that I might consider approaching in the financial services industry. Later that day, we did our first television appearance on a show called *ID Plus* on RTÉ, Ireland's national television and radio broadcaster. My friend Shane O'Neill had arranged this through his fiancée (now wife) Kathy, who works with RTÉ. It went well but yielded nothing for us in terms of sponsorship.

We were willing to try anything to get sponsorship. One day I was out on a training run when I nearly ran over a man who had just got out of a car. The man was Bono! I quickly sidestepped him and as I continued running, I began to wonder was there any way Bono could help us out, given that our chosen charity project was a pilot scheme for self-sufficiency in Africa.

About half a mile later, I had a brainwave. I turned around and sprinted as fast as I could back to our house, wrote a note for Bono, put it in a plastic sleeve and legged it back to where he had parked his car. The plan was to put the note on the car with my contact number. Bono would then call me, and I could explain what we were doing and ask him to help us publicize our row. Unfortunately, by the time I reached the spot where he had parked, his car was gone. Maybe he would have just laughed had he actually read the note, but I figured it was worth a shot – you don't ask, you don't get. By now I knew that this row would not happen if Tori and I didn't stick our necks out and weren't willing to take the rejection. I still have the note I wrote that day – I was actually quite impressed with it considering how rushed it was. I even managed to quote Nelson Mandela.

As the months wore on, we were starting to run out of time and getting desperate about where the money was going to come from. Would we have to scrap our dream because we didn't have enough money? It couldn't end this way.

Sponsorship proved to be the single most difficult aspect of the entire project. We sent out proposals to about 200 companies, most of whom did not even reply. Tori faced the same struggles in Canada, where she was trying for sponsorship, too. When she returned to Ireland in March 2005, she had a lot of numbers and one or two positive responses from her hometown of Devon – from the Lions Club and community Rotary. But, alone in Ireland for most of the early part of the year, I was finding it a very frustrating and difficult time. I had never worked as hard on anything in my life while getting so little in the way of results.

Frequently, while driving home from work on a Friday evening, I would look out my window with envy at the crowds of people, both young and old, smiling, laughing and chatting over a few pints after a hard week's work. It may sound silly, but these were difficult moments for me. I had worked myself to the bone throughout the week, trained hard and often woke up at my desk at home at three or four in the morning having fallen asleep writing up sponsorship proposals or researching equipment. I would drag my weary body up the stairs to bed wondering what I had got myself into. But there would be no let-up, no time for recovery over the weekend; this was our busiest time. However, this was our choice; this was our life now; this was our daily grind.

CHAPTER 10
The Daily Grind
SPRING AND SUMMER 2005

Tori ···

I told myself it was like being a Bond girl. Up at 5 a.m., then sweaty gym work for most of the next few hours. I came home at 7:45 a.m., showered and beautified myself. I switched from Tom Girl to Beauty Girl with the flick of a makeup pen. I would be ready by 8:30 a.m., at work and smiling in Jigsaw boutique for 9 a.m.

The hardest bit was walking out the front door at 6 a.m. It was like hitting a wall of freezing air. The cold seemed to cut right through my bones. We had already done half an hour of a Pilates stomach and core exercise routine. Now it was time for the short walk along the Strand Road in Sandymount to the gym. I knew the sea breeze would bring me to life, but on mornings like this it was still pitch black and absolutely freezing. The last place you wanted to be was outside.

We spent from 6 to 7:30 a.m. doing weights, then very small amounts of cardio work and Ashtanga yoga. Our objective was to gain strength and endurance, as well as body mass, particularly for me, as I only had eight stone to throw behind the oars. My workouts in the morning never lasted more than two hours; this was a religious routine for me. A girl has to have time to prepare for the day.

Both Paul and I worked full-time jobs from nine in the morning to seven at night; Paul sometimes worked up to 10:30 p.m. Both our jobs required us to be on our feet all day. This would take its toll.

Our house was like a produce farm; we had to be so health-conscious that year. We could not afford to let our immune systems break down, as we had so much ahead of us. We made fresh juice every morning before going to the gym, and after it we packed the carbs in with oats or porridge to set ourselves up to face the day. The girls at work made fun of me as I came to work every day with at least two full boxes of packed lunch. We trained so much that both Paul and I felt like we were starving all the time. I said at least 50 times a day, "Is anyone else hungry?" in a moany voice. My boss usually gave in and allowed me to quickly eat something just to shut me up. For lunch I had a bowl of soup, a pork chop with pasta and a salad. I tried to make everything from scratch to avoid saturated fats and preservatives.

The first thing I did when we got home in the evening was make dinner. We used food as a stress buster to try and control our temperaments. We were finding ourselves very fatigued. Eating unhealthily affected our energy levels, and we could not afford this.

After dinner Paul and I usually went back to the gym or for a walk or to Ashtanga lessons, returning home at around 10:30 p.m. Time to chill out? Not at all. We had the pressure of preparing sponsorship pitches, which we couldn't do during the day – we still had to pay the bills. We were up until three in the morning. More often than not it was Paul writing up the sponsorship proposals, as he was more familiar with companies in Ireland.

It was extremely difficult to sell our idea. Not many people really embraced us during this part of the game. I don't blame them. Two unknown people come to your company and ask you to give them money to row an ocean; they have no experience and no guarantee they will succeed. We knew it would take a special person to see past the obvious doubts. We knew finding this person would be like finding a needle in a haystack. Self-belief seems to be quite rare, and we needed to find companies who valued and recognized its power. They would know that self-belief is so powerful it would give us as good a chance as any to get across.

Usually I do not take much notice of the negativity I am faced with, but there were moments when it just seemed to build up on me and I felt worn out. I wondered if people believed that by discouraging us enough we might not follow through with the row. All it seemed to be doing was leaving friends and family dissatisfied and Paul and me exhausted while causing rifts in our relationships.

As the summer approached, Paul and I were under immense pressure. We were struggling to make the payments to the race organizers, to find the time to train properly and to keep friendships going. A few times a week the girls from work went out for a few pints. I felt guilty that I could not go along, or when I could I was not able to drink because I could not afford the beer or risk the hangover, in case it affected my training the next day. I was very lucky with my friends, as they remained strong for me and put up with me continually turning down invitations.

When it came to the row, Paul's friendships and mine were different. I had met some amazing people over the previous year who had been aware of my intention to row the Atlantic right from the get-go. They took me at face value and loved me and respected me for the adventurous person I am. There seemed to be no begrudgery. Paul, however, was up against history. His friends and family were genuinely worried. They had not been convinced from the start that he was this adventurous. They perceived this as a silly idea because it was so outside their own boundaries. Why would we put ourselves in so much danger? Any reward we perceived could not be worth the risk of losing a life.

Since they had no experience of these things, I think they saw this as an impossible dream, a death wish, if you like. It is only human nature to fear what we do not know. It comes down to different mentalities and perspectives on life. Probably neither mentality understands the other. I could see the stress this put Paul under, and occasionally it wore him down.

Paul had chosen not to let other people's boundaries or perspectives sway his decision. He told me about a quote that comforted him in his convictions. "Don't judge other people's capabilities based on your own limitations," wrote Jesse Martin, the youngest man to sail around the world solo. He too was probably up against the odds. When you know you believe in yourself even if others do not, nothing can stop you. We held onto the idea that this was probably what got him around the world and that we should respect our friends' and families' perspectives even if they did not understand ours; fighting them would only cause everyone grief. We just had to stick to what was in our hearts; only then could we push on. I knew Paul's determination would be one of the qualities that would get him across this ocean against the odds.

Paul

It was all starting to fall apart. I arrived home from work, exhausted after another hard week of training, organizing and work. As the clock entered the small hours of Saturday morning, April 9, I was still at my desk making out list after list after list of all the things we still had to do. The desk was a mess of papers, and my head felt like it was about to explode. I was completely wiped, but I could not go to bed until I made some sense of it all.

"Just draw up some plan to say that we can do it, that we can get everything done in time . . . if we save this amount each month, we can buy our water-maker on this date . . . no, too late, we need it earlier . . . oh, no, we still have to factor in food for the month . . ." Ahhh! I had never felt as stressed as I did at this moment. Even as I write this, the confusion returns; as I go through my notes and diary entries, it all seems like madness.

The months were on fast-forward, and we still had a mountain of things to get done. We weren't making any serious progress on the sponsorship front, but we just didn't have time; we needed to focus more on getting ourselves and the boat ready. We had a lot of fundraising ideas and events that we wanted to get off the ground for Concern, but there just didn't seem to be enough hours in the day. It felt at times that we were just going around in circles. We were chasing our tails!

In June the British and Irish Lions rugby team were touring in New Zealand, and this was my one little escape from the madness of the row. Every Saturday morning during the tour, Daragh, one of my roommates, and I would get up early and go to a pub that had the Sky Sports network on TV, usually Kiely's or the Merrion Inn, to watch the match. Once we stepped inside, I was lost to concerns about the row. For that hour and a half, I just enjoyed the rugby and chomped my way through a delicious Irish breakfast.

We had completed our sea survival course and our first aid at sea course in April. It brought home to us again that this was going to be a dangerous adventure. Deep down, I think the danger and the uncertainty of it all was part of the attraction for me. I think when we are outside our comfort zone and the safety blanket of society is discarded, that is when our spirit, our soul and who we really are kicks in. I suppose in a strange sort of way I wanted to push myself into this corner and see how I would react.

Christina was out of the water in Peter Kavanagh's back garden in Arklow. Every weekend we worked on her. The biggest structural change we were forced to make was extending her keel. The keel is a sort of fin that runs the length of the boat beneath the hull and helps direct the boat. *Christina* had a skeg, which was like a keel except it only ran half the length of the boat and tapered off at the end. Woodvale insisted that all boats competing in the race had to have a full-length keel, so we had to put one on. This required the considerable skill of a good boat builder. Peter, who has built many boats, including his own sailboat, took on the job. He spent many hours on it in his workshed and would not ask for payment. One sunny morning in the first week of June, we opened the door into Peter's shed and there she was, all equipped with a new keel. It was like Christmas morning for a child.

By now *Christina* was taking on a personality for me. She was the third member of our team. Peter had strengthened the keel with fibreglass sheeting, so Tori and I enthusiastically began paring down the fibreglass and sanding down the hull. "A messy job," as Peter said, smiling as he watched. Then it was time to paint anti-foul on the underside of the boat to prevent barnacles growing on her while she was at sea. Tori hated this – she said the smell of it made her toenails curl! But this whole exercise would prove crucial during the row.

Once the anti-foul was on, we flipped the boat over. There were at least ten grown men helping and we still struggled to flip her over. This was a big job done. We sanded down the remainder of the boat and painted her with the help of some friends. *Christina* was coming to life, looking brand new again. Watching the boat's transformation was like doing our very own *Pimp My Ride* show.

Rowers place their feet on a foot board when they row. Peter made a new one for the stroke position (the rowing position nearest the main cabin at the back of the boat). He also cut out the shape for the other foot board. I took on the job of finishing this one myself, not least because I had worked little with my hands since a bit of metalwork and woodwork at school, and Eamonn pointed out that this would have to change – I would have to fix things (we both would) if they broke when we were on the Atlantic.

The foot board problem was difficult because my feet and Tori's are very different sizes and we couldn't go with the obvious solution of sharing a pair of shoes mounted on the stand. Eventually I set about making up a temporary one on which we should be able to use our own runners and adjust straps to suit them. I needed to make slits in the board and find suitable straps. I walked into an old car scrap yard in Dublin and asked the man if I could have some old webbing or seatbelts that he didn't need. He looked at me suspiciously but relaxed when I told him what it was for and cut me a few yards. I then went into a fabric shop and purchased some velcro strapping. Next up was a little shoe repair shop to get the velcro straps stitched to the webbing. The straps needed to be attached through the foot board itself. I went home to Limerick that weekend and Dad helped me, as I had no tools at this stage. We didn't have a jigsaw so we simply drilled holes through the wood, one below the next, to make a long slit through which we could sling the foot straps. A few hours later we had a foot board!

I know many people might laugh but I was really proud of this little piece of workmanship. I was also very impressed that Dad helped me. Despite not wanting his son to head out into the Atlantic risking his life in a small rowing boat, he put these fears aside, rolled up his sleeves and decided to make sure I was well prepared. He is the best dad in the world.

We got another nice lift when we spent four days in Belfast at the International Yachtmaster Academy. The race organizers required us to do a course that included navigation by the sun and stars, so that we would have this skill if our GPS broke down. It was a joy to spend time in the company of Captain David Comer, a man who told us that for him the sea is the real world.

The time had come to put *Christina* in the water and row to Dun Laoghaire marina, where we would berth the boat and have easier access. This trip would be a big step for us. Could we complete our first significant passage on our own?

CHAPTER 11
A Maiden Voyage and a Flash New Car
JULY–AUGUST 2005

Paul ···

"By failing to prepare, you are preparing to fail." From here on in Benjamin Franklin's words carried huge meaning for us. We even had them up on our wall at home, along with other sayings that we used to help us stay focused.

It was time to use the knowledge we had built up, to take control of our rowing and take charge of *Christina* on the water. Our maiden voyage was to be the 65-kilometre (40-mile) trip from Arklow to Dun Laoghaire, and Eamonn Kavanagh asked us to draw up a passage plan. We should know the tides, be prepared for any changes in the weather and have all the equipment we needed. Up to now, we had been carefully supervised by Eamonn and Peter. Now we must cut the umbilical cord.

We would row through the night, starting on July 23, and Eamonn thought it should take about 24 hours. I could not believe the amount of equipment we loaded up. We had food and water supplies to last three days in case we got into trouble, a hand-held short-range radio, a mobile phone, wet-weather gear, a quilt, a sleeping bag, a radio, CDs and a player, and a camera to record the trip. We also had a navigation chart and our GPS, into which we had entered a series of waypoints for our passage. "There's nothing here you can do without," Eamonn said reassuringly.

The waypoints would help us break the trip down into smaller distances so that we would know exactly where we were and how far we had to go. At nighttime, when we couldn't see land, the waypoints would let us know what our position was, and should help us avoid Wolf Rock (outcrops partly submerged in the sea).

We decided to leave Arklow about two hours before the tide turned in our favour. The tide on the Irish Sea works on six-hour shifts. As it comes in, it runs north; going out it moves south. We wanted it running north with us but in the last hour or two of a tide it is at its weakest, and because we would be fresh at the start, we could pull against it. Leaving two hours before the tide turned should give us eight hours with favourable conditions. Eamonn told us that it was crucial we get around Wicklow Head as soon as we could. It is about 19 kilometres (12 miles) from Arklow, and if the weather turns it is no place to be in a rowing boat. Our plan was to give it socks for the first few hours, rowing together to get around the headland as fast as we could.

As we boarded *Christina*, Eamonn asked me to tighten the gates that hold the oars in place. He handed me two vise grips. "Make sure you don't drop them in the water, Paul," he said. I held them tight, as if my life depended on it. I was very excited, like I was a child again. Eamonn cut through the mood with ominous words: "If you get in trouble and have to call out the lifeboat, you can forget about using my boat in the race."

His logic was spot on. If we could not safely get to 65 kilometres north of here, how on earth did we expect to cross the Atlantic? He explained that even if the weather changed unexpectedly, with proper planning and judgment we should still be able to pull in somewhere or drop our anchor and let the weather pass. If we panicked and called out the lifeboat, then we had no business taking on the Atlantic. These cautionary words set the butterflies off, but I was also excited by the challenge – the gauntlet had been thrown down. I told Eamonn there was no way we would be calling on any boat to assist us; we were on our own now.

We set off from Arklow around 3:30 p.m., a little later than we had planned. I felt a huge buzz of both excitement and nerves; this trip had to run smoothly or our Atlantic dream was over before it had even started. For all intents and purposes this was our Atlantic, right here, right now.

We started off well and safely rounded Wicklow Head. We rowed together for about five hours and then we took turns, allowing each other to rest. However, because of our late start, the tide turned against us and we were still a few miles from Greystones, where we had planned to pull in for a few hours' rest to let the tide turn in our favour. The track wheels on my seat, which slide it up and down the rails, were broken and kept slipping off. This added to the frustration of pulling hard against a stiff tide and made for very slow progress. A slight northerly wind had begun to blow against us. We kept close to the shoreline and plodded along, arriving at Greystones just after 10 p.m. We were quite tired after nearly seven hours of rowing, but at least we were making progress.

"The Atlantic is going to be very hard," I thought, as we tied up. Eamonn called us on our mobile and congratulated us for getting as far as Greystones. I think he was happy that when the tide turned against us we kept slogging away rather than dropping our anchor. This is the mentality that we would need on the Atlantic.

We slept for a few hours and pulled out of Greystones shortly after 4 a.m., when the tide had turned in our favour. I was very surprised by how refreshed I felt after just a few hours' rest. The conditions were good; we rowed well together and arrived into Dun Laoghaire just after 10 a.m. Eamonn called us as we entered the marina and asked if we were we still in Greystones. I proudly told him that we were just arriving into Dun Laoghaire. He congratulated us on making our first successful passage. We cautiously made our way into the marina, avoiding the other boats. This was the first time we had rowed *Christina* into a marina, and the last thing we wanted was to ram into somebody. We pulled into our berth, which was one of the emergency bays right in front of the marina office. Mission accomplished!

We were delighted with ourselves. Although we both felt a little tired and hungry, the training we had put in over the previous few months had stood us well. *Christina* was happy in her temporary home, which had been donated free of charge by Hal Bleakley, the general manager of the marina in Dun Laoghaire. Completing this passage was a very important step in terms of gaining the respect not only of Eamonn and Peter but also of our friends, family and others who may have thought we were not up to the task we had taken on.

Having the boat in Dun Laoghaire meant we could train virtually every day, and we could work on installing the necessary equipment. But we didn't have enough money. Funnily enough it was some good news that brought this home to us. Dr. Laurence Swan of Fyffes called to say they would help us out with our shipping costs with a sponsorship cheque for c$7,500. I sat down to see what effect this would have on our overall finances. My heart sank. We would have to get a bank loan. It was too late in the day to be relying on sponsorship that might or might not come in.

Even if we got the loan, it would not solve all our problems. A friend, Donagh Nolan, visited Dun Laoghaire and watched as I listed all the remaining jobs to be done on the boat. "You need to quit your job straightaway and work full time on this," he advised. He was right. I had planned to finish up work in early October, but this would have been too late. Tori and I decided that I would be the one to quit my job, although financially this was a big blow.

Before I quit, I needed to get the loan approved. We needed c$45,000. I wondered if I should tell the bank what the loan was to be used for. Because I see banks as quite conservative when it comes to lending money, I decided to say I was buying a new car – a 3-series BMW. Nervously, I sat opposite the lending adviser, and when he asked what the loan was for, I enthusiastically produced the *Car Buyer's Guide* and showed him the car. We both agreed it was a fine car and proceeded with the application. I received a phone call the following day that the loan had been approved. I jumped for joy and rang Tori to tell her the good news. We would now definitely get to the starting line.

We were still under serious pressure to get all the remaining work completed on the boat before shipping it, but the financial reins had been loosened – at least for now. The next day I told my boss I would have to leave my job earlier than planned. Marc Evans, my manager at Cornmarket, and all the other staff were good about it, as they had been ever since I'd announced my intentions nine months earlier. They all thought I was daft, but they were very supportive. I really was lucky to be working with such a good bunch of people at this stressful time.

And so began the last mad sprint to get everything done on the boat in time. *Christina* was due to leave Ireland for shipping to the Canary Islands via the UK on Saturday, October 8. But, as usual, we were up against it in terms of time.

CHAPTER 12
A Sprint for the Line
SEPTEMBER–OCTOBER 2005

Paul ···

Time. We never had enough time. The starting date for the race was just months – and then weeks – away, and there was always another thing to do, another mad dash to collect something. Each night before going to bed, I sat down and wrote out a list of things I had to do the following day and a time for each. We were on the homestretch now, and we would soon begin to see light at the end of the tunnel – or so I told myself. It was easy to forget what we had accomplished each day and just move on to the next thing, so I made a point of physically ticking items off my list at the end of every day so I could feel a sense of achievement.

Some things I just couldn't do on my own. The water-maker, which turns seawater into drinking water, would be the most important piece of equipment on the boat, so we had taken most of the c$9,000 I got from my last bonus at work and bought the best one we could find – a Spectra Ventura 150. I was intent on fitting it myself, but when I took the measurements I could not see how to install it without some amateurish hacking at the boat. Every boat builder in Dublin seemed too busy to take on the job, but after a bit of hounding, Edwin Brennan agreed to come down and look at what needed to be done. When he arrived, I wouldn't let him go until he agreed to do the job. He also advised us on fitting a new hatch and splash rails for the forward cabin. The splash rails, I think, were a complete waste of time but the organizers insisted on our fitting them.

Edwin and his father, John, were brilliant, and they allowed me to study their methods in case I needed to fix anything at sea. We needed electrical work done, too, and Edwin put me in touch with Tony Brown, a hugely knowledgeable and very clever guy, who made everything work – and spotted that the solar panels we had would not be sufficient to recharge our battery given our estimated power usage. We managed to source an extra solar panel from the UK. It cost us a fair bit of money to get the help of professionals like Tony and Edwin, but it was money well spent. Their work would stand up to everything the Atlantic threw at us.

When it came to our food, race rules stated that you had to have enough food for 90 days, but many teams were taking just 60 days' worth of full food supply and 30 days' half supply to keep down the weight of their boats. We were aiming to do as well as possible, but we were 99 per cent sure that we would not win the race. We decided to put safety first and take a full 90 days' supply. Looking back now, thank God we did.

Before we ordered the food, we ate a sample order for a week straight to make sure it did not upset our stomachs. Our food was all freeze-dried: you simply added water and, *voilà*, dinner was served! Our breakfast would be porridge and muesli, while our main meals were potato-, rice- or pasta-based meals, such as beef stew, cod and potato casserole and, my favourite, pasta bolognese. For the trip, we decided to pack our food into daypacks, so that each day we could open a package and know that would be all the food for the day. These daily packs would be important to help us ration the food and safeguard against eating too much early on in the race when our bodies would be crying out for food. We also had energy bars, biscuits and cup-a-soups. We would buy chocolate bars and other treats in the Canaries when we arrived. Over a few late nights, our housemates, Daragh Brehon and Miriam Walsh, helped us package all our food. We used a bilge pump to suck the air out of the packs and so save valuable space on the boat. By now our rented house was a complete mess, cluttered with all sorts of equipment and food.

We also roped Daragh and Donagh in for some on-the-water activities. We needed to test our water-maker at sea, so we rowed out from Dun Laoghaire on a rough day with the two of them on board. In this busy area we needed to know there would always be someone at the oars, and, as we had no water ballast in the boat to keep it deep in the water, our two friends acted as human ballast! Testing the water-maker was crucial. On the ocean, this piece of electrical equipment would supply us with water for drinking, cooking and washing. It would suck huge amounts of seawater – it discards about 90 per cent of its intake – and take the salt out of it. If air got into the system, it would cause the water-maker to break down, and ideally it would have been installed in the centre of the boat, so low that the inlet hole would remain submerged even in rough conditions. Because Eamonn and

Peter Kavanagh had strengthened *Christina* with a second floor and foam padding between this and the hull, our water-maker was not at the lowest point. But when we rowed out a mile from Dun Laoghaire and tested it, everything worked fine. This was a huge relief.

The time had almost come for *Christina* to be shipped out. The two other Irishmen taking part in the race, Gearóid "Gags" Towey and Ciaran Lewis, who were very helpful to us, had generously lent us their trailer to transport the boat to Antrim, from where she would be shipped to England and on to the Canaries. The day before I drove her up, I met Eamonn Kavanagh in the car park of Dun Laoghaire marina. He brought us a spare set of oars, a survival suit and a box of honey for the trip. He looked over the boat, all done up and fully equipped for the voyage ahead for the first time since we had taken control of her, and seemed impressed. I breathed a sigh of relief.

I had never towed a boat before, so, after checking that everything was properly tied down, I tentatively edged out of the marina in Dun Laoghaire before dawn. I reached Antrim at nine. I watched as the guys in the depot pushed her around as they loaded her into her container. They couldn't be spending much time on this because they had a lot of work to do, one said. Oh, no, we won't have that! We had put over a year's work, blood, sweat and tears into getting to this stage. After a few firm words, everyone at the depot found time to make sure *Christina* was safely secured for her trip. I was almost paranoid: I went back to the boat three times to double-check everything. Then I patted *Christina* on the gunwale, wished her a safe trip and said I'd see her out in the Canaries. As I headed back toward Dublin, I had a moment. Holy shit! We would make the start line. In a few weeks we would line up with 25 other boats from all over the world to row across the Atlantic Ocean. The race start now awaited us. La Gomera, in the Canary Islands, here we come!

Tori ··

It was finally time for us to fly. A year of hard work, dedication and old-fashioned sweat and tears had paid off. Up the stairs of the plane I walked. La Gomera awaited us. As I sat down and reflected on the last year I could see the faces of the family and friends we had left behind, and there was a bittersweet taste. We were so excited to finally face our adventure, but to see the people we loved in pain was difficult. And we were the direct cause. We could prevent their pain if we would only give in and give up our dreams, but we were selfish.

A few days earlier I had run up to my room almost in tears: I had asked some of Paul's friends to write him encouraging letters to boost his spirits throughout the race, but they did not seem to take the request seriously. One of Paul's friends said, "Just give him a piece of cheese." It's an in-joke between the boys, but I took it as a cop-out. I was not asking for a joke but a bit of support for Paul, and as usual the boys missed the point on the sentimental stuff. Due to the pressure I was under I took this personally. I felt that, down to the last minute, even some of our friends were not taking us seriously. Only as we were walking out the door did they see the penny drop. "Holy shit, they are actually going to do this!"

This did not hold for Daragh Brehon, who is one of Paul's closest childhood friends, and Miriam Walsh, together our housemates. They were our most genuine supporters right from the start. So when it was time to go, we did not want anyone else to take us to the airport.

We headed off at about four in the morning to Dublin Airport. There was a chilling silence in the car. It was surreal to me that after the longest year of my life we were actually leaving. As we checked in I felt like it was all coming too quickly. Time seemed to be fast-forwarding. I turned around to see Mir's eyes welling up with tears, and that was it – I was beyond control. It was as though my face started to flood, and my tear ducts exploded. I grabbed Mir and embarrassed her with the most genuine hug I have ever given anyone.

Tough old Daragh started to well up as well, but he was hoping nobody was looking. I was, and it meant the world to me. It felt so unnatural to be leaving them. They were like my Irish family. I felt like they should be coming on the row with us: over the year they had gone through every up and down; they knew just as much as we knew about the row. If someone was curious about the row they would often call Daragh or Mir instead of us. They saw us go through the sponsorship rejections and the family reactions. They stayed up till all hours of the morning helping us pack our food and organize the orders. They put on fundraisers and promoted us to anyone who would listen. Most of our publicity came from Daragh's Friday nights – to put it lightly, he has the gift of the gab. Whoever he could rope in heard our entire life stories; bless whoever was sitting next to him. Dar and Mir even put up with seeing their living space become a boatyard. Looking back at it, I don't know how they did not throw us out. Throughout the row, we would both think a lot about Dar and Mir and realize just how much their friendship meant to us. If not for their support, we might not have made it to the start line.

As the plane took off, I came tumbling down to reality. I could actually die on this row, I thought. I was 21, and contemplating my mortality had never crossed my mind before. We had been too preoccupied over the last year to stop and just think about this. I could feel my stomach churning. This was a crucial moment for me. I made a mental commitment that it was not going to happen. I would not let my mind go there. I reminded myself that I am not a realist but an idealist. The best quality of my personality is that I have not lost the self-belief you have when you are about five years old, at a time when the world has not yet got you down. Why think negatively when you could be thinking positively? I made a choice to keep myself on a positive cycle. My mortality was out of my control so why worry about it? What I did have control over was living life, living it to the fullest. So I made a decision to just go for it.

As the plane landed in Tenerife, there was a sense of self-satisfaction I had never felt to this extent before. As we entered the tiny airport, I could not stop myself looking at others around me and wondering if they were here for the race. I must have been creeping people out! I was staring at them wondering who was a parent and, thrillingly, who was a rower. Immediately, four girls caught my eye. They definitely had to be rowers; no one brings that much luggage on a sun holiday. I wondered if they were professional rowers. How long had they been training? Why were they doing it? It was all so exciting, I could not wait to meet all these people in the weeks ahead.

We flew out with Gearóid Towey, one of the other Irishmen doing the race. On the ferry ride to La Gomera, Gearóid's sister, Jeanette, was ill throughout the 30 minutes. I thought it was a good start that none of us who were taking on the Atlantic was sick, but until then I had never seen seasickness up close and it did not look pretty. I just prayed that I did not get it when the row started.

La Gomera turned out to be a quaint and friendly little Spanish island. After we landed I stopped to watch the passengers disembarking. I knew it! The four girls I had seen in the airport were there – they were introduced to us later as an all-girl crew. We stayed in the centre of La Gomera at the local *pension* (hostel) with a beautiful veranda and quirky Spanish shutters. It was just the way I wanted to spend my last few weeks on land, as it might be a while before we hit terra firma again. The owner was an old Spanish man who I imagined as a mob-type character with an Al Pacino vibe. He showed us around the hostel, his belly hanging off his small frame and a cigar the size of a sausage dangling on the end of his lip, the ashes catching on the first few buttons of his shirt. Every time I walked past this greasy little man he would mumble in Spanish under his breath. I prefer not to know what he said, as we thought of him as our little Spanish daddy for the next few weeks.

The first night there, I was sitting in the window looking out when the four girls I had seen passed the hostel. One of the crew, Sally, yelled up to me to ask me if I was a rower, as if I was she wanted me to come down to the Blue Marlin. This was a great little local pub and the unofficial meeting place for Atlantic rowers in previous races. Sally had taken part in the race already and was going around the tiny village inviting everyone down to the pub. I practically jumped out the window and had a pint in my hand and Paul in the pub with me before I could even tell him what was going on. Many ideas and friendships would be born in this little pub. It is a place I will think of every time I think of the row, as all the rowers have left their stamp there over the years.

I was on a mission to find a small Canadian flag for the boat. My mom had sent me one about half the size of Canada, afraid that I might be mistaken for being Irish. Since our boat was only 23 feet long and the flag covered half of it, I realized I could not use it. We could be penalized for having a sail! As I walked into the pub, there was the flag I needed hanging from the ceiling. It was meant to be; it was waiting for me. After a few too many pints I wandered back to the hostel to collect my Canadian flag as I had decided – though the Blue Marlin did not know it – that we were going to trade flags. Manuel, the bar owner and a character in his own right, informed me that this flag had lived in his bar for nearly 20 years. But it was just the flag I needed, weathered and smoke-stained. I could tell it was seaworthy and had years of life experience and stories behind it – that it was what I needed. It would get us to Antigua: there is nothing like old-fashioned Canadian spirit to have on your side. Manuel gave in, took the flag from the ceiling and signed it for me. He then hung the new flag up, so that in 20 years someone else can come along and trade their flag for a more innocent one like mine. And that is the stamp I left in the Blue Marlin.

The following day we headed down to the boatyard to find *Christina*. It was surreal to see all the other boats; they were so sexy-looking with their sleek demeanours. However, the first thing I noticed on *Christina* was the wood trim, and I thought, "This is a boat that looks seaworthy." When I studied the other boats they seemed too cool, as if they might be made of plastic. *Christina*'s air of confidence and life experience reminded me of a Harley Davidson; she was built like an ox. The other boats looked as though they were built for speed, maybe like the Japanese racing bikes with good aerodynamics, but who knows how they would take a fall? My dad is a Harley Davidson man and I was reared a 100 per cent Harley girl. He used to wear a T-shirt that said, "I would rather eat shit before I would ride Jap crap." As inappropriate as this might have been, I saw Dad's T-shirt in my mind's eye and knew I trusted *Christina* to take us across the Atlantic, even if she was a little on the heavy side.

I could not believe how beautifully fitted out the other boats were, with fancy music systems, guardrails, and insulation on the inside of the cabins. All the boats were supposed to be of the same specifications, but I could swear the insides of their boats were bigger. Some of them actually looked like different boats. And many of the support teams seemed to be like little armies. One team had 30 people! There were marketing and public relations managers, charity representatives, boat builders, documentary teams – the list was nearly endless. It was at this moment that Paul and I sat back and realized we might be in over our heads. We did not have anything structural to organize on the boat but the little things seemed to take up our time. There were moments when I felt like asking if I could borrow someone from another team's entourage. Really, did they need 30 people? Surely one person would not be missed? We had to sort everything out ourselves, running around this little island like chickens with their heads cut off.

Our Spanish was limited, so trying to find the right supplies was like engaging in a game of charades. After a morning of chasing around, one of us would get back to the boatyard and the other would almost assume they had found everything except exactly what was needed. By the time we would head back to town, siesta would have started. We would have to wait through the afternoon in the slumbering village. I love the concept of siesta, but it just was not practical for our purposes. We wasted so much valuable time waiting for this town to fire up. Even after siesta, it was like the town was still asleep. At times I just wanted to scream WAKE UP! Meanwhile, several of the other teams did not even have to come down to their boat, as their boat builder or their team were organizing these things for them.

Our boat was berthed beside *Bout de vie*, the crew of which would become the most respected team in the race. Frank Bruno and Dominique Benassi were both amputees, each having lost a leg in an accident. After meeting them I came to doubt the accuracy of the word "disabled." They did not let their "disability" hold them back in life, and their strength of character and strength of mind were such that not for one moment did it ever occur to me that they were not the equals of everyone in the race. Their self-belief and obvious steeliness came across as they took their boat apart one day, completely disassembling the hatch of their bow cabin. As with our boat, *Bout de vie* had been used first in the 1997 race, and we had faced the same problem with our hatch months before. It had taken us weeks to find a solution and in the end we had paid a boat builder to fix it. These men obviously knew what they were doing if they could fix theirs in one day. Wow!

Bout de vie had a seaworthy look to her and a remarkable story behind her. She had been built by French prison inmates and had been successfully rowed across the Atlantic in 1997 by Joseph Le Guen and Pascal Blond, a man who had just been released from 14 years in jail. I am not sure if I would want to be in a boat with a convicted double murderer for any period of time, but fair play to Monsieur Le Guen.

Meeting Frank and Dominique put Paul and me into an upward spiral of inspiration. We met Mick Dawson, who is like the Wayne Gretzky of ocean rowing, and he was such a positive force I immediately ran down to the little call centre, as I needed to talk to anyone to just get this energy off my chest. I felt so alive. I felt like I was going to explode, I was on such a high in the company of so many dreamers.

So many people like me. Nothing could be outrageous here. After a year of negativity, it was so refreshing to be surrounded by people who could understand why someone would want to take on a task like this. It was almost dangerous in their company – who knows what ideas we could come up with if we all put our heads together. I spoke a hundred miles an hour to my mom. I just could not express my emotions quick enough. I had found my niche. I knew I was meant to be here and that this row was for me. My mom just giggled on the other end of the phone as she tried to take in all the emotion and inspiration and youth in my voice.

I talked to my mom almost every night. When I look back, this must have been like torture for her. She was thinking, "Would you just go already so you can get back already!" However, I eased her anxiety as I told her of how the organizers, Woodvale Events, were assisting us. They were not going to let us go out into the Atlantic unprepared. They set up a scrutinizing system and came around to all the boats. They tore through the boat, from stern to bow, making sure we had all the right equipment and that we knew how to apply it. Some teams had to undergo scrutinizing three or four times, with each lasting a minimum of two hours. They gave us some of the most useful advice and tips we received. Mick Dawson was part of this team and was particularly helpful as he suggested putting our collision flares on deck for easy access and a trip line on our sea anchor. He helped balance our boat properly to reassure us that we would self-right if she were to capsize. The scrutinizers provided that little boost of confidence and reassurance we needed from a professional and experienced crew of people. I felt as ready as I was ever going to be to face an ocean.

Paul ··

The Blue Marlin pub was packed with rowers. I gave Manuel the nod: "*Dos cervezas por favor.*" We were in company with Gearóid Towey and Ciaran Lewis, the other Irishmen in the race. As I passed a beer to Tori, Gearóid introduced us to another rower, James Cracknell. After a brief handshake, we exchanged a few minor pleasantries. Cracknell partnered Ben Fogle, a BBC television presenter, and they had become known as the celebrity team. As we all chatted away, the mood was good, and the conversation pulsed through a pub full of dreamers who were about to take on the might of the Atlantic. As I looked around our little circle, it suddenly hit me. James Cracknell was a two-time Olympic champion, Gearóid was a former world champion and an Olympic rower himself, Ciaran was a seven-time Irish rowing champion – and then there were Tori and me! We were amongst some of the best rowers in the world, and we were, for all intents and purposes, novice rowers, set to take on perhaps the most difficult rowing challenge on the planet. But, for some strange reason, it felt right. Not for a minute did I feel like we didn't belong here. "This is great, I'm loving it, I think I'll have another beer. Manuel . . ."

Tori ··

I was introduced to James Cracknell. He looked me up and down. "Are you on the support boat?" Now I know he is a very prestigious sports person, but who did he think he was – assuming I was on the support team just because I was not a big, buff, "GI Jane" character? Our boats were only two down from each other in the boatyard. It was so obvious that I was participating in the race, as I had been fixing and organizing the boat every day. Did he think I was doing it for fun? I bet he thought I was down here to support my boyfriend. I felt my blood start to boil. In the two seconds it took him to ask this question, a million thoughts ran through my head. I know I made a mountain out of a molehill, but I saw red for the lack of acknowledgement he gave me while showing all the men in the pub respect. He totally offended me with his arrogance, and what's worse, he had no idea. With piercing eyes I told him, "I am rowing this ocean as well, thank you!" And I swiftly moved along.

Paul

All day we prepared. Every once in a while I would look around, and it was hard for us to see all the other teams with so many friends and family around, while we were on our own.

My heart was really torn here. My sister was living in Bahrain, so I knew she couldn't be with us for the start of the race. I spoke to my parents about coming out. I thought it might have helped ease their concerns if they came to La Gomera, met some of the other rowers, their families, the support crews and the people involved in the race. I think they understood my logic, but the overwhelming image from all of this would have been them standing on the dockside seeing their son row into the unknown. I think this is the image that would have remained with them throughout the race and might have been too much for them, causing them even more worry. So we decided it was best for everyone if they did not come out to the start of the race.

Although I understood this, it still hurt a little when I saw other rowers with their families on their boats and going out to dinner with them in the evenings. Maybe because most of them came from rowing backgrounds, they naturally had support from friends and family, as they had a genuine interest in the race. For us, even on a practical level, having a few extra pairs of hands around would have been a big help. But I could see things from my parents' perspective. Because Tori's parents and her brother live so far away in Canada, they too were not able to make the start of the race.

La Gomera is beautiful. The people are friendly – very natural and laid back – and the island is relatively untouched by tourism. A week before the race we put our boat in the water and then walked up to the supermarket to buy our 150 litres of fresh-water ballast. This supply would be packed into our centre compartments on the boat so that if we did capsize during the race, the weight and positioning of this water should help self-right *Christina*.

What Paul and Tori Wore (or Didn't) on the Crossing

For most of the Atlantic crossing, Paul and Tori rowed naked. Sweaty, wet shorts can become encrusted with salt on an ocean row and lead to painful chafing. They had sheepskin covers on their rowing seats and the natural fibres helped avoid wear and tear on their rowers' skin.

They sometimes wore a pair of rowing shorts when it was wet and the waves were breaking in. The sheepskin covers became soaked through and seawater can be cold. After a long time rowing in the sun they wore T-shirts to combat sunburn.

I was asked to move our boat around to the other side of the pontoon. Tori had gone back into the village for more supplies so I set off on my own. When you row you always have your back facing the direction in which you are moving, so I was constantly looking over my shoulder to avoid hitting anything. Nice and steady, everything was going fine. But as I began turning *Christina*, she continued to glide through the water; she wasn't slowing down as quickly as before, maintaining her momentum much more now as a result of the extra weight provided by the water ballast. The boats were berthed two and three deep, and I was now ploughing straight for another boat, *Sedna Solo*, Roz Savage's boat. With many of the rowers looking on, I rowed backward as fast and as hard as I could to stop *Christina*'s momentum. Luckily enough I just about slowed her down and one of the other rowers (Frank Bruno from *Bout de vie*) saw what was happening and gently nudged *Christina* away from Roz's boat. God, that was nearly very embarrassing. Ah well, I thought, there's plenty of space where we're going!

Eamonn and Peter Kavanagh arrived in La Gomera a week before the start of the race. This meant a lot to us. To think that the only Irish people who had rowed an ocean had come over to see us off was overwhelmingly uplifting. While Tori worked on *Christina*, I met the lads at the ferry and brought them straight to the boat. Peter hadn't seen

Christina since we'd rowed out of Arklow over four months before. We spent the next hour or so chatting by the boat and Eamonn and Peter said she was well set up. Peter gave us the same Irish flag they had used on their crossing in 1997, and I proudly put her up straightaway.

Despite our blatant inexperience, I felt very confident about our preparations. We knew what we were doing and were ready to go. Obviously the Atlantic would test us beyond all our known limits, but I genuinely believed 100 per cent that we could do it. I had no doubts in my mind, and Eamonn and Peter commented on how relaxed we seemed.

The following day, our mood quickly changed when we discovered we had left the charging mechanism for our iPods back in Ireland. These would be our only constant source of external entertainment on our long journey. We didn't want to lose our music selection. We took the ferry to the nearest big island, Tenerife. A company in Ireland had told us that if we could access a specific type of camera equipment they would fashion our images into a documentary when we got home, so we went looking for that equipment too. But after trying every decent electrical shop in Tenerife, we still had nothing. Our iPods were quite new and neither they nor the chargers were in the shops in Tenerife. Nor was the camera equipment.

We sat on the side of the road, our heads slumped into our hands. It was dark and it was time to catch the last ferry back to La Gomera. I let out a deep breath, screamed a few obscenities and wondered could anything ever just be straightforward for us? Why did every single detail with the row seem to cause us so much hassle? Tori broke down in tears. I tried to console her, telling her it would all work out, but I had the feeling my words carried very little reassurance for her. At this point it looked like we would be rowing across the Atlantic without our music selection; and our chance of making a documentary on this, the adventure of a lifetime, was disappearing fast. There wasn't much said on the Fred Olsen ferry back to La Gomera.

I called our friend and housemate Daragh and he located the chargers at home. The relevant shops in Dublin were out of stock of the camera gear we needed. So that was a problem we probably couldn't solve. But how could we get the iPod chargers to La Gomera? A courier could not guarantee delivery on time so we needed to find somebody to fly out to the Canaries with them. I told Daragh that if we had to, we would pay for him to come out with the gear. It was that important to us. I also called Dad for help. After a few days of frantic inquiries, he came up trumps: Ron McPartland, a good friend of his and a retired Aer Lingus pilot, arranged to have them brought out on a flight. I'll never forget the moment when I checked the chargers on the boat to see if they worked. It was about 10 p.m. and the red "charging" light lit up. I have never felt more relieved.

The race was to begin on Sunday, November 27, and we went to the official pre-race party on the Friday night. The atmosphere was good and everyone was more or less ready to go. However, Mother Nature was about to play her first hand. The effects of a tropical storm out in the Atlantic meant that it would be too dangerous to start the race as planned, and it was postponed until the following Wednesday, November 30.

We were disappointed but knew it was the right call. Unfortunately, however, it meant that Eamonn and Peter, along with some of Gearóid and Ciaran's supporters, would miss the race start, as they were sched-uled to fly back to Ireland on the Tuesday. We all went out for dinner, the last supper so to speak, on the Monday night. We walked back to our hotel to collect a few things that Eamonn and Peter were bringing home for us. I handed our bag to Eamonn, shook his hand and told him I would swap him this bag for his boat in a few months' time. As Peter turned to walk away he paused, smiled and gave us the thumbs up. "You'll be all right, we'll see you again," he said. I thought I noticed a slight welling up in his eyes. I felt quite choked up myself. It was, I feel, a vote of confidence in us. He was telling us we wouldn't die out there. It meant a lot to us and strengthened our resolve to make it across the Atlantic. Eamonn and Peter are two of the finest people I know, and I feel honoured our paths have crossed. They are two tough men, the type of people whose respect you have to earn, but they were absolutely fantastic to us and we couldn't have asked for more support. I think we saw the softer side of them in the Canaries.

On the day before the row I made one final attempt at locating camera equipment. There aren't many people in this world who get the opportunity to document the biggest adventure of their life in this way, so it seemed worth a try. The plan was to take the morning ferry to Tenerife and be back for dinner with Tori, Gearóid and Ciaran and their group that evening. The morning ferry was cancelled, so I boarded the midday one and spent the next eight hours running all over the island, sometimes jumping into taxis and out again at the next shop. I had no luck and my last run was a sprint to catch the last ferry back to La Gomera. I was completely dejected; my evening meal was a ham sandwich, a small box of Pringles and a can of Coke on the half-empty ferry. Poor Tori was wondering if I had missed the ferry altogether. This wasn't the way I wanted to spend my last day but there was nothing I could do. Tomorrow was game time. We could hardly sleep that night. It was something we would soon get used to.

Tori ⋯⋯⋯⋯⋯⋯⋯⋯⋯⋯⋯⋯⋯⋯⋯⋯⋯⋯⋯⋯⋯⋯⋯⋯⋯

Finally the start. After a year of anticipation and a delay from the tropical storm Delta, the day was here. I just wanted to get on with it. The wind was blowing and the waves were crashing over the wall of the marina, yet I still wanted to be out on the ocean. I had "fight or flight" symptoms – the feeling in your stomach when you know you are about to do something dangerous. I took it as a good sign that my first instinct was to fight; to get going. Hopefully this would stand me over the next few months.

I went to bed the night before and lay there looking up at the ceiling, trying to imagine what could lie ahead for me. What was my destiny? The only anxiety I felt was because my rowing partner and boyfriend was not there with me.

I had spent my last day alone as Paul had left the island to try to find camera equipment for a documentary. We knew we would not be able to get it in La Gomera, as mere bolts and screws seemed hard to find. That evening I dined with Gearóid Towey, Ciaran Lewis and their group. As night fell, the thought kept crashing through my head: what if Paul hadn't caught the ferry? He would miss the start of the race and we could be disqualified. Rowing on my own could not be an option. Could it? I felt so relieved when Paul finally arrived back, even without the equipment. If he had been any later I would have started mentally preparing myself to row the ocean on my own.

On the morning of the race I was surprisingly calm. I got out of bed at about six o'clock to make sure we did not leave the last of our belongings behind. I put on my rowing shorts, knowing this would be the last time I would be publicly clothed for a few months. It was like preparing to enter a nudist colony. We said goodbye to the old man from the hostel who had been our imaginary support over the last two weeks. I pretended he was family, and it gave me comfort to know someone was there for us, someone to watch us take off into the distance.

Down I went for breakfast, for my last Spanish omelette. Breakfast over, there was nothing left for us to do but go to the boat.

There was an amazing feeling in the air. As we walked across the square down to the marina, I spotted Gearóid's mother, Carmel, a genuine and gentle woman. Along with Gearóid's sister, Jeanette, she had gone out of her way to wish us well. Carmel embraced me and the hug was as sincere as my own mother's would have been. I could feel their anxiety, and tears welled up in Jeanette's eyes. What we were about to put our most loved ones through was evident; I felt very selfish. But the show must go on.

We walked down the pier. First there was the all-doctor team of Becky Thorpe and Steph Temperton, who called themselves *Making Waves*. I wondered if we would beat them. What was their fate? I approached them with a hearty handshake and good wishes. We had met amazing individuals over the previous few weeks and had bonded with them. There had been so much camaraderie in the air, it had been a truly original experience. We all felt we were one team and now we were going off on our own adventures and would probably never see each other again. Through sharing this experience, we had developed some lifelong friendships in a short space of time, friendships that we felt would last long after our Atlantic adventure. Some people were doctors, some boat builders, some sailors, some carpenters. The list is long. So many people from so many different walks of life – it was bizarre to think everyone would return to the lives they had put on hold over the previous year. They would go their separate ways and might never cross paths again. But even if we never physically saw each other again, I knew we would all share this experience as a lifelong bond.

The next team was *Mark 3*, crewed by Robert Eustace and Peter Williams, two of the soundest lads I had ever met. Paul and I really bonded with them, as they were the only other team that were not really racing but had taken up this challenge for an experience. They were so easygoing, with the right, laid-back approach to life. There had been a few beers shared over the weeks, and this was the only team I was certain I would keep in touch with.

Finally we reached our own boat. I was surprised I still felt relatively calm. I almost felt I should be starting to panic a little. Had I really comprehended what I was about to attempt? Out loud, I said, "Tori, you can blag your way through many things but this could be life or death. Are you ready for this?" The people on the boat next to me were looking at me a little funny. I replied to my own question, "You're as ready as you're ever going to be. Tori, you do not regret the things you do in life but the things you do not do. So chin up and push on."

I should have been going over every nook and cranny in the boat, but if I had found anything wrong I might have fallen to pieces. I was calm on the outside but my emotions were as fragile as the shell of an egg. It would probably be fair to compare me to a pregnant woman; I was trying to hold myself together but swinging up and down like a yo-yo. I felt like everyone was looking at me, waiting for me to crack. I wished my mom had been there with me in those last few minutes as I tried to comprehend an experience bigger than anything else I had achieved in my life.

I had already driven myself crazy over the previous few days checking the boat. I realized I had one last moment to be girly and looked down at my legs. I could not bear the thought that I would not be able to shave over the next few months, so I thought it would do no harm if I waxed my legs one last time to preserve a little femininity. I headed up into the little village of La Gomera for the last time and into the beauty parlour. The women looked suspiciously at me as I played one last game of charades to make sure they did not take the wrong hair from the wrong places. They looked at my rowing shorts, probably wondering why I was giving myself beauty treatments an hour before I put myself into total seclusion in the middle of the ocean. It was part of a sanity thing, to delay looking at jungle legs for as long as possible.

Back down on the pier, Paul was walking around the boat ranting and raving. The organizers were trying to give us a time penalty by making us start at the back of the fleet because Paul had not attended the last safety meeting. This was a real kick in the face. Realistically, due to the level of competition, we knew we would probably end up at the back of the fleet anyway, so it did not matter where they started us. Maybe it would have been better to take the place they gave us and not say anything. But there was a principle at stake: we had complied with the organizers' requests with no hassle and then they threw this at us. It was almost like they were trying to take advantage of the little guys. We put our foot down. With our nerves running high, it was actually dangerous to throw something like this at us. One of us just might have flipped the lid. The celebrity team (James Cracknell and Ben Fogle)

Steering on Christina

The steering system consisted of a T-bar in front of Paul and Tori's feet. This T-bar had ropes coming from each side of it that were connected with the rudder. The rudder, which is below the boat, controls the direction of the boat by moving from side to side.

On *Christina*, Paul and Tori had the option of jamming this steering line in the jam cleats, which would hold the T-bar in place and so lock the rudder in a certain position. Jam cleats are small holders for a rope or other cord.

showed up a week late and totally took the piss. Just because they were celebrities it seemed nothing had been said.

In the end, all the teams were scattered across the imaginary start line. One of the crew from the support boat was in a rubber dinghy calling the boats out one by one. He passed us about three times before giving us the go ahead. I was so excited I had to distance myself from the situation to keep a cool head and stay focused. I played a game of pretending I was just rowing around a pond: what is the difference between a pond and an ocean anyway?

Most of the teams left the marina quite smoothly. There was a group of spectators, and having never had an audience before, I was a little nervous. When we set off for the mouth of the marina it really was "all eyes on us." I rowed and Paul stood controlling the rudder to guide us between the boats. It was a tight squeeze and there was not much room for error. The weight of the water ballast made it quite difficult to control the momentum of the boat; a mere tap on the oars could really send her flying. We were headed straight for a sailing boat, and I tried frantically to back our boat up. A young Scandinavian couple sat on the sailing boat cheering us on. They had this sort of clueless look. They had no idea we were about to plough right into the bow of their boat. "They might not cheer as loud when they realize what is happening," I thought. I could feel my face burning with embarrassment. "Show everyone you belong here, Tori," I said to myself. "Take control of the boat! If you cannot row her out of a marina, good luck rowing her across an ocean." This little pep talk charged up the stubbornness in me. "You are 200 kilograms and 2 metres tall," I told myself. In my head, I was probably the biggest person in the race – of course I could control the boat. I found the strength to bring *Christina* to a halt. Then all we had to do was head for the mouth of the harbour. We were sorted.

There was a sense of freedom as we looked out at the open ocean and the unknown. I had never felt so alive. Nothing had ever felt so right. My intuition told me this expedition was meant for me, no matter what the outcome was. My heart was pounding and I could feel the pulse in my veins. It was pure adrenaline. The feeling of ecstasy was such that I understood how people get addicted to adrenaline rushes. I was so proud of myself and Paul. It had been a crazy year of hard work and dedication and the reward was finally upon the horizon, within arms' reach.

All of the teams were so eager to get going, it was like trying to hold back a herd of charging bulls. I could just taste the adventure in the air. Behind us I saw Gearóid and Ciaran exiting the marina and heading into the deep blue sea. They pulled up beside us. I felt a huge sense of camaraderie and truly hoped they had an adventure of a lifetime. I also hoped we would finish around the same time. It would be great to see them in Antigua!

CHAPTER 16
Seasick

Tori ···

I yelled over my shoulder to Paul to pick up the pace. The rolling swell pushed at us as we attempted to keep up with the world-class rowers. I was sitting in position one, at the stern of the boat, and it was the first time I had used the rudder, which steered the boat. One of the women from *Mission Atlantic* shouted out, "Bearing 240!" I had no clue what she was talking about – how was she going to keep an exact bearing? The way the rudder worked, when I pushed forward with my right foot the boat turned to my left; push with my left and it went right. I was having trouble getting this into my head. We were only ten minutes into the race and we had already almost collided with one of the other teams. I tried to correct and went straight for them instead. We were literally zigzagging off the start line.

The adrenaline was unbelievable. I could feel the blood pumping through my veins and my heart pounding like a drum. The rolling swell was about 2 metres deep but felt like 7. It was the biggest we had ever seen. As the waves came toward the boat, we paddled as hard as we could, trying to surf them. At first we tried to race the other boats; it was not long before we lost sight of them. We were really racing the waves. The water was absolutely beautiful. I was in control of my surroundings and positive about what lay ahead of me.

Exactly three hours into the race, Paul let out a small moan from the back of the boat. In a shaky voice he said, "I am not feeling that great." I said, "Oh, come on, you will be grand, just do not think about it." Two seconds later Paul's face turned a mossy shade of green. This was like something you see in cartoons but not in real life. I thought his head was going to explode; he projectile-vomited over the side of the boat. I would say every person within five miles heard Paul's heaving. Sweat coursed down his forehead and saliva dripped out of his mouth. He clenched himself into the foetal position, his head on the gunwales. His body went limp, as though the life had just been ripped out of him. It disturbed me to see Paul in such a vulnerable state.

Paul

This was a truly horrendous feeling. I had never been seasick in training, so I really didn't expect it. I just wanted to curl up and die, but I had to keep rowing. My routine for the next day or so consisted of puking and rowing, with very little food staying down. I became dehydrated and felt very weak and dizzy, but I knew it would pass and was determined to keep rowing. To think that I actually paid a lot of money to do this!

Tori

I was so worried about Paul. When someone is seasick there is nothing you can do to help him; you just have to wait for it to pass. On the second day of the race, Thursday, December 1, we had our first interview, live with Ed Myers on Live 95 FM, a local radio station in Limerick. Paul could barely hold on to the oars; he was swaying from side to side as he rowed. He was more or less stirring tea. The last thing he wanted was to sit and talk to someone on dry land, to be asked why he was doing this. Not very good timing. I only had to look in his eyes to see that at least part of him thought this was the worst idea he had ever had. But he did the interview. I felt deep admiration for him. Paul felt like he was about to die and still continued to row his regular shifts. Not once did he ask me to cover for him. All he had been able to eat in the last 24 hours was Egon's bread (special, slow-release, gluten-free bread given to us by a friend of Eamonn Kavanagh's) and some sweets. Thank God for Egon Friedrich's bread; without it I feared Paul would have burned out by now!

As the night approached, we saw the boat *Gurkha Spirit* rowing in our direction. As the crew, Al Howard and Nick Rowe, passed by we exchanged a few words. Paul and I had not rowed last night but now I didn't feel so guilty – apparently a few others in the race were seasick and did not row either. Even I was starting to feel a little woozy; that morning I could barely stomach my ready-made porridge. With every bite I could feel the porridge fuel my body while my stomach attempted to reject it. "Mind over matter, mind over matter," I kept telling myself. I was trying to convince myself I did not have seasickness. Possibly I was starting to feel sick just because I was seeing Paul so ill.

Paul only managed to eat half of his meals, I did not know what he was running on. Throughout the first day we rowed our two-hour shifts up until midnight. I could see Paul just did not have the strength to go on. He came into the cabin and told me the drogue bridle (the ropes holding a kind of wind sock that is thrown into the water behind the boat to stop it moving side-on to the swell) looked like a yawning dog or a massive snake with its mouth wide open and about to eat someone. I went outside and had a good look at the bridle. I just could not see it. I knew it was probably time to call it a night. I would not have minded rowing, although I was feeling pretty vulnerable, if not quite hallucinating. The reality was that we were going to fall behind if we did not row at night. I felt very guilty and I wondered what our mentor, Eamonn Kavanagh, must be thinking. The course we had chosen was to go south as fast as possible and so pick up the northeast trade winds, which should help us move west and south. Eamonn could watch our progress on the website for the row. I hoped we were not letting him down.

We slept together in the cabin that first night. At four in the morning I woke from an awful dream: someone had their hands around my neck. My head felt dizzy and I was disoriented. For a moment I could not figure out where I was. I had totally forgotten about the row and wondered why I was not in my bed at home. I frantically grabbed Paul, who reached for the cabin door. As it flew open I could feel the hands release my throat and I could breathe again. We must have used up all the oxygen in the cabin. This is the worst nightmare for anyone who has a fear of suffocating.

On day 3, after making breakfast at around 5 a.m., Paul and I started rowing together. We decided to do this all day to pull back some ground. By three in the afternoon we spotted another team, *Moveahead*, not too far from us. We had to beat these guys; they were my friggin' parents' age! For the next ten minutes we were in a race again. We turned the engines on and strode past the boys as they had a cup of tea. I felt good and strong inside – this was my first mental boost. We turned on the music to *Braveheart* and lost sight of *Moveahead*.

I wondered why we had not seen any marine life. I was sure we should have seen something by now. Come on, even a fish would have excited me. I was a little bored. But then, I might have cared a little more if I were not so exhausted.

Our routine for the next 60 days or so would be very simple. One of us would row for two hours while the other rested. This system must be maintained 24 hours a day. The two hours on, two hours off routine had been the tried and trusted method for pairs ocean rowing for years. Before the race we experimented with other shift lengths but settled on the two-hour one, as it worked for us. Our two hours off would be spent sleeping, eating, fixing something, doing our weekly updates with the media or writing up our diaries.

As night rolled around I turned on my iPod and listened to an audio book: *The Distant Echo*, by Val McDermid. I was determined to get past midnight tonight, maybe even through the whole night. Trying to stay awake was so foreign to my body, it felt like a Chinese torture. Outside the cabin, when night fell, it was as though someone had turned out all the lights. I was the captive of the mysterious deep voice on my audio book. It was probably not a great idea to listen to a murder mystery on my first night shift. I was shit scared. When I was seven years old my brother told me there were ghosts downstairs and then locked me into the basement. The terror I felt then returned now, as I sat alone in the middle of the ocean. I was surrounded by the unknown. I really wished I didn't have such a wild imagination. I was counting down the minutes until my shift was over. Paul climbed out of the hatch. His turn must be up. Wahoo! I was off my seat like lightning and into the cabin, my safe haven. Paul was wondering what the hell was going on. I wouldn't allow myself to listen to that book at night any more.

I lay in the cabin on the cold leather cushions. The night was cool. I expected it to be a little bit warmer. Between the temperature and the cabin rocking from side to side, sleep seemed impossible. I heard a bang on the deck – Paul had been knocked over by the swell. We decided to call it a night and tie down the steering lines so that we did not go too far off course.

DAY 4, DECEMBER 3, 2005

When we woke at 7 a.m. it was nice to see that the steering lines had held. It was Saturday, December 3, day 4 of our odyssey. I checked the GPS: we had drifted a little farther west than expected. We had planned to go south first to catch the trade winds, but we were not worried because we had to go west at some point anyway. Today we would get back into the routine of each of us rowing two hours on and two hours off. We could not have maintained any stamina if we had rowed together all the time. The swell was a little bigger today at about 3–4 metres, coming from the east. There was a good force 5 or 6 wind pushing us west, which made getting south hard. The boat was moving fast, almost surfing the waves. I rowed as hard as I could to make up ground. I was dreading nightfall when the waves start to pick up.

I expected big seas but I did not think there would be big breaking waves that would rush at me so fast! In the middle of my night shift I heard a familiar sound. It sounded like a steam train coming. What in God's name could that be? Bang! A rush of icy water tumbled down on me. It was so cold I think my heart stopped for a second. A wave had broken over the side of the boat. All of a sudden the waves had changed their course. When I looked out at them they seemed angry, distrustful. I got to the cabin and pondered how I had actually signed up willingly for this.

Paul had got over the worst of the seasickness, but after an hour of rowing he was very uncomfortable with this weather as well. We were probably being a little over-cautious, but in fairness this was the biggest swell we had ever rowed in and it was coming at us from all sides. The swell was now beginning to push us northwest, so we threw out the drogue, which is meant to keep the boat straight. We certainly didn't want to go too far north. Even though we didn't row we didn't get any sleep. I could hear the rudder banging on the boat as the rope slipped out of the jam cleats. It was so loud it sounded like the back of the boat was going to rip off. Every 15 minutes or so we took turns to reset the lines. I had a feeling we had missed a big opportunity to make some serious miles during the night with such a fast swell behind us. Eamonn advised us to just go with the weather even if the direction was not due south.

The next day was Sunday. The support boat pulled up beside us. I felt a little embarrassed; they probably thought we were barely rowing. They had heard about Paul's seasickness, and Lin Parker, the skipper, wanted to know how he was. He had eaten a whole meal today; he was back in the game and back on form. According to Lin, some teams kept rowing the previous night: they went northwest but when the wind turned, it would get them farther south. Shit! We should have done the same. Life is about living and learning. Tonight we had to row no matter how uncomfortable we were; we just had to get on with it or we would not complete the row in 60 days, which was our target.

Our rowing was a little smoother that day, and there was a gentle northwesterly wind. We felt we could do 50 miles over 24 hours if we rowed through the night. Before the first night shift, the two of us fell over laughing. We were in hysterics, for no apparent reason. This lightened our mood and reminded me that it was not all that bad out here. Paul was trying to do a freshwater flush to keep the water-maker clean and unclogged but nothing was happening; we would investigate further tomorrow. Over dinner, we decided to change our schedule to get us through the night. We agreed we had been stupid to think we could just keep rowing through the night, with no breaks and no food. Every hour, we would allow ourselves a small break for a biscuit, and at midnight we would stop and have a cooked meal. If I made it through the night I would reward myself and call my mom the next day. But only if I got through the entire night.

There was a beeping in the cabin and I traced it to our satellite phone: "Message received." I did not know we could receive text messages. Wahoo! The message said, "Hi guys, watching progress. Hope you are getting your sea legs. You are doing great. Love you both. Mom (Fran)"

I felt so touched knowing Mom was watching. I could not wait until the next day to tell her I had made it through my first night of rowing. It was amazing how much I had thought of her over the past few days. I had never realized before how much I relied on her support; she truly was my rock. I wanted to make her proud. It was a clear night and I sat rowing, looking at a perfect dome of stars. And then two shooting stars lit up the night sky. On the first I wished we would make it to Antigua safe and sound in 60 days. On the second I was more ambitious. Eamonn and Peter Kavanagh did it in 58 days and four hours. I wished for 55 days. Maybe we could beat their record!

CHAPTER 17

Sea Anchor

Tori ··

The sleep deprivation was killing me. I thought I would be used to it by now. Mick Dawson of the organizers said that after a week or so the body would adjust: mine was rebelling, saying, "What are you doing to me?! Give me sleep, sleep, sleep." The night shifts pushed me to my limits, and I was starting to realize that Eamonn Kavanagh was not exaggerating when he described the row as a prison camp. What had I got myself into? I was hitting my first emotional wall. I expected the mental and physical tiredness – but why was I so weepy? In my head there was a voice saying, "Do not allow yourself to be the weak link. Do not let Paul down; he is relying on you. No one thinks you are capable of this; do not prove them right." When I told myself this, it spurred me on and I made it through the night shifts. But every night, it seemed to be that little bit less effective. My spirit was slowly plummeting; emotionally I felt I was about to hit a bed of rocks.

Paul knew it was time to put his hand deep into my bag of treats. He pulled out a letter. It was from my beloved daddy, who had always helped me through the hard times in life. His letter was so appropriate now that I needed to call up my inner strength. As I curled up in the cabin I found myself resorting to the foetal position. Maybe this was a subconscious comfort position. I held the letter tight to my chest. I read the words I knew would push me across this ocean:

> [You] know just how proud we are of the great success, values and accomplishments of our children. Both your brother and yourself, mother and I have insisted that you think on your own, gain and use knowledge wisely and keep your eyes open to the world . . . You have both succeeded beyond our fondest hopes and wishes . . . You have come of age [and] it is a pleasure to observe you making decisions in your life, some we don't quite understand but they are your decisions and having helped you become

> capable of rational thought we respect and attempt to
> understand your dreams as an adult. Don't worry, you will
> always be my little girl.

In this moment it was as though my dad was sitting in the cabin with me. I could hear his voice, and I even knew the way he would read this letter: leaning back in a chair with his glasses precisely placed at the end of his nose, far enough down that when the tears in his eyes started to well up, the rim of his glasses would catch them before they slid down his face; then maybe no one would notice. Dad, I always notice. I continued reading, thinking hard about every word Dad took the time to write down. I needed to embrace his words of wisdom and take responsibility. I made the choice to partake in this challenge. I was not raised to be a quitter. As I approached the end of the letter I had to pass it over to Paul, as I was blinded by the storm brewing in my eyes. I was deeply moved by my dad's love for me and his faith in me. I knew I would return again and again to this letter through the row, and through my life. Even Paul's voice started to quiver as he read the end of the letter.

> Yes, you are the master of your destiny. Some stinky old
> beer-drinking biker said that. Don't know why, just that
> some beautiful, bright-eyed little girl needed a little help
> to nudge her on the way, to create and live a life others
> could only hope to read about and make their most secret
> dreams of.

As Paul embraced me I felt a deep sense of gratitude toward my family that I had never openly shared. Even though they were an ocean away I had never felt as connected to them as I did in this moment. Nothing would get me down with them protecting my spirit.

Dad added a PS: "Be nice to the little Irish fella. You may have to eat him."

DAY 11, DECEMBER 10, 2005

The weather had been strange, the ocean presenting an eerie calmness, but now the winds began to blow us to the northeast. This was exactly the direction we intended not to go. It was truly heartbreaking to be

Sanitation at Sea

The toilet system for ocean rowing is called "bucket 'n' chuck it." The bucket was kept in the forward cabin at the front of the boat and emptied as necessary. Urine was collected in a small bottle adapted for the purpose. This was left empty on the deck near the stroke seat rowing position so that when either of the rowers needed to go, they could just grab the open bottle, do the business, chuck the contents overboard and resume rowing.

After going to the toilet the rowers had a dry hand-wash that contained disinfectant. Most mornings after breakfast Paul and Tori would wash their faces and their teeth. They also brushed their teeth after every meal because electrolyte and energy drinks can be hard on teeth.

They only showered twice during the whole row, once at halfway and once just before they came into Antigua. Why so little? Water was scarce and they were mostly too exhausted to bother.

trying so hard and going virtually backward. Paul and I decided we would not row that night and reassess the weather in the morning. We knew that at some point we would have to use the sea anchor. But this was only day 11!

We were facing into winds of force 3 to 4 on the Beaufort scale. The scale goes from zero to 12, with zero being flat calm and 12 a hurricane. Force 4 was the equivalent of a wind of about 20–30 km/h (12–19 mph) with a moderate breeze. Ordinarily, this would not present a problem except that it was now blowing straight in our faces, and because of the size and weight of our boat and the surface area of the cabin, it was extremely difficult to row into any decent sort of a wind. If we were on a training run and had only a few kilometres to go we could slog it out. But over a sustained period of time in the Atlantic Ocean, trying to row into this would be just a waste of energy. According to a text from the support boat, we could expect force 7 to 8 soon. Force 8 was gale-force

The Beaufort Scale of Wind Speed

Beaufort Number	Equivalent speed at 10 m above ground		Wind name	Observable wind characteristics
	knots	km/h		
0	<1	<1	Calm	Smoke rises vertically; sea like a mirror.
1	1–3	1–6	Light air	Smoke drifts; ripples on sea.
2	4–6	7–12	Light breeze	Wind felt on face, leaves rustle, vanes moved by wind, small wavelets on sea.
3	7–10	13–19	Gentle breeze	Leaves and small twigs in constant motion, light flags extend, wave crests begin to break.
4	11–16	20–30	Moderate breeze	Dust and loose paper raised, small branches move, fairly frequent white horses at sea.
5	17–21	31–39	Fresh breeze	Small trees sway, crested waves on inland waters, moderate waves at sea.
6	22–27	40–50	Strong breeze	Large branches move, telegraph wires whistle, foaming crests and some spray at sea.
7	28–33	51–62	Near gale	Whole trees in motion, inconvenience felt in walking against wind, foam at sea begins to be blown into streaks.
8	34–40	63–74	Gale	Twigs broken off trees, walking upright difficult, wave crests break into spindrift.
9	41–47	75–87	Strong gale	Chimney pots and slates removed, high waves at sea with rolling crests and dense spray.
10	48–55	88–102	Storm	Trees uprooted, considerable structural damage, sea appears white with high overhanding waves and streaks of dense foam.
11	56–63	103–117	Violent storm	Very rare on land, causing widespread damage, sea covered in foam patches with waves high enough to hide medium-sized vessels and with crests blown into froth, visibility affected.
12	>64	>118	Hurricane	Sea completely white, with driving spray, the air filled with foam and spray, visibility seriously impaired.

conditions with winds up to 63–74 km/h (39–46 mph). In these sorts of conditions we were going nowhere.

Paul threw down the sea anchor, and I was not sure if we were going parachute jumping or stopping the boat. A sea anchor is basically like a big parachute at the end of a 50-metre rope. The line is tied to the bow (front) of the boat and thrown into the water. The parachute opens up underneath the surface, catching the water and so adding drag to prevent the boat from being pushed backward.

We had not planned it this way but we had our first unbroken sleep of the row. The novelty of an eight-hour sleep was unbelievable. I felt human again. However, by morning we had gone 3.7 kilometres (2 nautical miles) north, even with the sea anchor out. This was disheartening. I looked outside to see the waves crashing over the cabin. They were the biggest waves I had ever seen in my life. The sea-anchor line looked as though it was going to snap, such was the pressure of the ever-increasing swell. Every time a new wave rolled aggressively under the boat it was as though the boat jumped to the next wave, leaving tension on the line. Paul called Lin Parker on the support boat and we were relieved to find out that all the other boats were on anchor, so we were not the only ones losing ground.

"This must be what it is like in the middle of a washing machine," I thought, as we tumbled around the cabin. Every time a wave crashed on the top of the cabin I instinctively ducked. How silly I felt. Drops of water began to leak into the cabin. We had never had this problem in the rain back in Ireland, but we were never out in this sort of rough weather. The leaks should not be dangerous but they were disconcerting and annoying. Drip, drop, drip, drop. The sound tortured us. The air was so moist from the condensation, this was like the worst camping trip ever.

I was surprisingly calm considering we were in the middle of the ocean in very rough conditions. Maybe it was because I was so focused on the fact that for the last four hours I had needed to pee. Every time a wave rocked the cabin my bladder was having convulsions to the point where it actually felt painful. I had to face the unforgiving wilderness, or, if there were such a condition, I would have internal peeing.

I tried to time when I was going to stick my butt out, and opened the cabin door a sliver. One wave, two waves, and here we go: full-fledged nudity on the horizon as my ass hung from the door. I had no choice but to just pee on the deck. I had never tried so much to force myself to urinate. Then it was like the never-ending pee. Paul was completely grossed out. It was surely not the worst act he had seen me commit, as he had just spent 12 days downwind of me, but this was too much for him. I was not too worried about the sanitation, as the waves crashing over the boat would eventually clear everything off. What would we do about number two? We drew the line at aping my last act; we strapped on a harness and made what felt like the walk of death to the other end of the boat where our bucket was stored. When we got there we held on for dear life.

We lay in the cabin. It was dangerous to go outside. This row was like a fish bowl, and all my little imperfections seemed to be magnified. I have had this freaky obsession with recycled air since I was a little girl, and I was prone to claustrophobia. In the middle of the night I woke up with an overwhelming sense that the walls had started to close in. I felt I was going to suffocate to death. Paul was taking in all the oxygen, and I was just getting all the recycled air. I was breathing carbon dioxide. I gasped for air, but my breaths were deep with no oxygen. I frantically reached for the cabin door, not even considering the dangers of opening it. I breathed again. Every two hours or so I would press my face against the glass of the door, open the latch just enough to squeeze my lips out and suck in as much oxygen as possible.

I knew our only option was to sit out this weather. I remembered a few words of wisdom from Peter Kavanagh: "This too shall pass," were the last words he said to us before leaving La Gomera. Our only option was to be optimistic.

I decided to open a few presents from our friends and family. One was from our housemates, Daragh Brehon and Miriam Walsh. They obviously had a situation like this in mind when they bought our present. How could a young couple occupy their time confined in a small cabin for days on end? The obvious answer was – Connect Four! I beat Paul again and again. We both had winning spurts, but I was in the lead.

During breaks from our Connect Four marathon we played Hangman using actors, countries, movies and singers. I am a really bad speller, making this very difficult sometimes. When boredom really took hold, I found myself staring at and examining everything. I looked at my hands: Wow, they really looked like my mom's hands. I had never noticed this before. I held a picture of my dad in my hands and I could see my face. I found this comforting. I focused on Paul, counting the freckles on his back or examining the fleck in his eyes. I was like a hawk with super vision; nothing got by me.

I had never had a period in my life where I took the time to genuinely stop, with no agenda. I realized it was such a great feeling to not be totally caught up in life, to be free to acknowledge everything around me. I felt I should be bored but was totally intrigued by this new pair of eyes I found myself looking through. Maybe the row was going to be a great experience after all.

When I first saw the cabin, the thought of being stuck in there with another person seemed incomprehensible. Now, I was completely comfortable and content to wait out this rough weather here with Paul. I felt we were in a safe little cocoon. As our sign said outside the cabin door, "Home Sweet Home." When we shut the cabin door, it was like shutting the door to the world. I knew that the wild winds and huge seas outside would eventually pass. When they did, we hoped we would have paid our dues to the ocean for the rest of the trip. Eamonn and Peter were only anchored for a few days on their trip. It would probably be the same for us.

Paul ···

DAY 13, DECEMBER 12, 2005

We got stuck on sea anchor right through day 12 and day 13. I was really frustrated by it. We knew it would be part of the trip, but we both just wanted to get going. We turned the phone on around dinner time on day 13 to check for text messages. It started to ring. Wow! Somebody from the world outside had actually got through to us. It was my mother.

"Paul, I'm afraid we have some bad news." She had awful news. I could hardly stand; I tried desperately to keep it together, but I broke down in tears. "I'm OK. I'm OK," I told my mother. Dad came on the phone. "If you ever needed a reason to finish this row, you have one now. Do it for Lynda." I said yes, he was right, and hung up. Tears again. Sobs and more sobs. I had not cried like this since I was ten years old. Tori held me, her eyes showing her worry. "What's wrong?"

Bevan Cantrell's mother, Lynda, had died very suddenly. Bevan is one of my best friends and Lynda was like a second mother to many of us growing up, always there at our rugby matches to support us and to rib us if we weren't putting it in. Lynda was one of the warmest, most charismatic and supportive people I have ever known. She was the type of person who instantly brought a smile to your face when you met her. Lynda suffered a brain hemorrhage and died within a few short days.

Even as I told Tori, I just couldn't believe it. I looked out on the horizon as the sun went down, and I was heartbroken. God only knows how the family were feeling; I called Bevan and his father Niall to sympathize. I could hardly keep it together. I told Niall our row was now in his wife's honour and with that again broke down in tears. Even now, as I write these words, I have a lump in my throat. Her funeral was one of the biggest ever seen in Limerick. It reflected the esteem in which she was held. But we couldn't go – we were at sea.

By the following morning the rough weather had passed. There were light winds and the swell was against us, but we reckoned we could make progress, albeit very slowly. The swell put pressure on the sea anchor, and I had a good 20 minutes' tug-of-war with it before I hauled it in. Every few seconds the ocean would pull sharply on the rope, ripping it through my hands. I cursed myself for not putting a trip line on it.

I dived under the boat to check for barnacles and shark damage. Everything was clear and there wasn't a shark in sight. Both of us had woken the night before and heard something rubbing up against the boat. We thought it might have been a whale or a shark.

The knock-on effect of spending days on sea anchor was that we had interrupted our sleep routine. Just when our bodies were getting used to the pattern of two-hour sleeps, we had found ourselves with nothing to do but sleep. We felt fresh, but we were facing a night where we had to start all over again. My first two night shifts were OK, but the final shift, from 5 a.m. to 7 a.m., was pure torture. It felt like time was moving backward. After what seemed like 40 minutes, I looked at my watch – 5:10 a.m.! "Dear God, this is going to be a hard one," I thought. It's a very difficult thing to fight. Your entire body and mind are crying out for sleep; everything is telling you to close your eyes. Your eyelids feel so heavy it is like somebody is standing on them. I was try-ing everything to stay awake, talking to myself, listening to all sorts of "pump it up" music, making stupid animal noises – you name it, I tried it. I struggled on, but by 6:20 a.m. I just couldn't keep going. Although I still had 40 minutes of my shift to go, I was spent. My engine was running on vapour and there wasn't a petrol station in sight. I set about taking the oars in to tie them down on deck.

As I took the second oar in I noticed a little bird hovering in front of me, just off the port (left) side of the boat. In that moment I imagined this bird to be Lynda's spirit, urging me on. Most of my friends call me Pucka, and I could hear Lynda shouting, "Pucka, put those oars back in. Come on! You can do it! Only 40 minutes left." I was a schoolboy again and Lynda would not let me flag. The oar I had withdrawn lay on deck, not yet tied down. "Bollix! Maybe I should try to keep going," I told my tired brain. One of the songs from my iPod had a phrase, "There's no easy way out," and it rang in my head now.

I lifted the oars, put them both back in the water and finished my shift. I felt great. This shift had been a huge struggle right from the start, and I had got through it. I had come up against a brick wall and managed somehow to find a way through it. This was significant, an important lesson for me at this stage in the trip. My mind raced back a year to Eamonn Kavanagh's words on the first day I met him: "This race is about how mentally tough you are." I could now appreciate fully what he meant. I also knew then that no matter how exhausted I became on this trip, I could push through it. The body would follow the mind and if my mind was right, I could push through anything. This night was a small victory for me, and although I would be up in two hours to do it all again, for now all I could think about was how good my next two hours' sleep was going to be.

We covered about 75 kilometres (40 nautical miles) that day, which I was satisfied with, considering we were rowing into a slight breeze and swell. However, it's funny the way your mood can change so much in a short space of time when you are at sea. The next day dragged big time as we struggled in the hot sun. For some reason, I just felt totally unmotivated and very tired. But while I struggled in the morning, by the afternoon I was fine. I had begun to listen to Tori's audio book, *The Distant Echo*, by Val McDermid, on her iPod. It was gripping stuff: a story about four Scottish students who discover a murdered young woman and become prime suspects. Life was so simple for us on that boat; the smallest thing could offer such immense pleasure – not a bad way to live your life.

Over the next few days we moved south, to around 22 degrees 30 minutes north of the equator, ever closer to where we should pick up the trade winds. But closer to the equator meant closer to the relentless sun. Throughout the day it stole our energy. Night meant very little rest or sleep but more work to make more progress. The mind must again overrule the body. The wind and swell now seemed to be turning against us. This was very worrying. Tori was feeling down, so I became Postman Pat and gave her a letter from her brother, Clayton. Although it lifted her spirits, it also stirred the emotions and freed up some tears. Neither of us was prepared for how emotional we got at sea, what a rollercoaster it could be. One minute a complete high, the next feeling like your world was collapsing around you.

Our little bird continued to follow us. She had appeared when Lynda passed away, and Tori and I became convinced she was carrying Lynda's spirit. "Hey, Lynda is back again," we would shout to each other when we saw her. Who knows, maybe there was such a thing as reincarnation. I thought she was keeping an eye on us. Unfortunately it seemed she could not do anything about the weather. The wind and swell were picking up in strength, making progress very difficult. The swell was about 5 metres (16 feet) high and coming at us side-on. We struggled on and did our best to keep making our way forward, but I felt that soon it would be a vain fight. Pulling hard on the oars but doing only a couple of kilometres an hour or even less was hard to take. As darkness fell each evening, we took consolation from the fact that at least we were still making forward progress, and we kept telling ourselves that it was probably the same for everyone else. This was a great driving force for us; we did not want to put the sea anchor out in case others were managing to keep going. Was this childish, or simply our competitive nature coming out? I like to think it was the latter. We could not see other boats, and we knew we would not win the race, but we both wanted to finish as far up the race rankings as we could.

DAY 19, DECEMBER 18, 2005

Despite our best efforts, by 11 p.m. on day 19, Thursday, December 18, we were starting to be pushed backward. We were forced to put the sea anchor out again. We were very downhearted. Our 60-day target for completing the race was disappearing. Mother Nature was deciding how long it would take us to cross this ocean. As I threw the anchor out, I realized that we had to begin to mentally adjust our target for how long the row would take. Simon Chalk, the managing director of the organizers of the race, partnered George Rock in rowing across the Atlantic in 1997. They initially felt they had a chance to win but realized a few weeks in that this wasn't going to happen. Simon told me it was one of the most difficult things of the whole row.

We had set our 60-day target logically and based it on times we were doing in training. You move quite slowly when rowing across an ocean, and there is a huge need to break the overall target down into ones for smaller units: months, weeks, days – even hours. These smaller targets kept us going. So when we were forced to change all this, it required a new mindset. We did not want to let a setback get the better of us, but it was very important to be realistic. To set ourselves an unrealistic target could be dangerous – we might be deflated if we did not reach it and find it difficult to go on. Hard targets might be good but only if they were attainable.

We sat looking up at the magnificent night sky and felt downcast. I thought of the old expression "Reach for the stars and if you land on the moon, what harm?" For now, all we could do was study that moon and those stars and hope things got better.

Tori ···

This just got harder and harder. We had struggled to make the water-maker work, we had put out the sea anchor and now the winds and swell had turned on us again. I did not understand this. Eamonn and Peter Kavanagh rowed this race in 1997, and Eamonn said they were only anchored once, for a few days. I thought we had paid our dues. I felt stubborn. I was not going to let the ocean get the better of me. But even rowing at full speed, the wind caught the cabin and we started to go backward. It was relentless. Our sea anchor plunged into the water again. We took to our cabin to sleep.

I awoke abruptly to the buzzing of the satellite phone. It was a text from Lin Parker on the support boat with a cyclone warning! What the hell was a cyclone? Two seconds later the phone beeped again with the definition: winds turning in a clockwise rotation. I did not feel so guilty about my ignorance; there must have been a few other teams who were clueless as well for them to send out a definition. We spoke to Lin, and she said that 18 other boats were on sea anchor. She was expecting the weather to change around lunchtime. Our fingers were crossed. There was nothing to do but just hold on until the winds changed.

We waited for lunchtime and it felt like waiting for Christmas. I peeked my head outside and conditions were still completely against us. I felt very naive at that moment. I was expecting the weather to turn exactly when the clock struck 12 because Lin said it would. If it did not, I thought I would almost have felt slightly betrayed, as though she had told a small child a lie.

Paul called Gearóid Towey and Ciaran Lewis in their boat, the *Atlantic Challenge*. They were approximately five days ahead of us, at 21 degrees north, 27 degrees west. We needed to hurry up. I really wanted to finish close to them. It would be such an accomplishment, as they were both world-class rowers. Those poor men! Whenever I imagined them cramped together in a cabin this size I felt a little humble. At least Paul and I were small.

Paul was cooking lunch now. I was going to wash out our sheep-skin seats for the first time. I had started to get a little chafing on my butt in the last few days, and I was hoping a cleaner surface would help prevent it when we got going again. I dipped the covers in a bucket with a little disinfectant. The water turned dark – I could actually see the salt concentration. We had been sitting on that naked! It put me off my lunch. I decided I was not going to eat that day, to ration the food, as I had a feeling we were going to be out here a lot longer than we first suspected. To dry the sheepskin, I strung up a line from stern to bow and fed it through the holes in the covers. I was quite pleased with my problem-solving. Hanging the seats would prevent them from getting splashed. This would allow both sides of the leather and fur to dry evenly. I was so proud of my mini-achievement, I decided to give myself my first shower of the row. Ah, bliss! By mid-afternoon the deck had been cleaned and my body and clothes washed. What else was there to do on a rowing boat but row? We were going to take in the anchor and at least give it a go. Maybe if we rowed together for a few hours we would make a little progress against the weather and gain an advantage on the other teams. It seemed like a genius idea.

With all of his might, Paul started to pull in the 50-metre rope, and it didn't seem that hard – until the first 2 metres tore violently back through his bare palms. Paul jumped around holding his hands. Was this a new version of the Irish jig? I left the cabin to go onto the deck. It looked like we might need a foreman. Paul pulled on some gloves and grabbed the rope again. A few seconds later the rope shot away, ripping his gloves open. Was that steam coming out of Paul's ears? "Should have put a fucking trip line on," he muttered. Eamonn had advised us not to put a trip line on the anchor because he figured it would just tangle in the anchor so it might not deploy properly. His advice was to just pull it in manually; apparently this had worked well for them. By take three, Paul had figured out that he could haul the rope in three waves at a time. He wrapped the slack around the side of the bow, so when the water caught the anchor again this held the rope in place. It was a sensible solution, if a little time-consuming. Twenty minutes later the 50 metres of rope had been pulled in and only the parachute of the anchor remained. Paul put one foot on the side of the boat and tried to pull the anchor and about 250 litres of water onto the deck. I walked over to him. "Pretty heavy, eh?" I confidently pulled one of the lines to collapse the parachute. Easy peasy. Paul pulled in the rest of the anchor. He wasn't saying much. I had a little snigger.

Our rowing gear was on; we were saddled up and ready to go. The push of an ox drove through my legs. Heave one. Heave two. Heave three. The boat had hardly moved. We stopped for a few seconds to catch our breaths. We lost the small bit of sea we had gained. I really did feel we were going to make ground with the two of us rowing. Half an hour later, it was apparent that there was no way we were going anywhere. We reluctantly threw out the anchor again and sheepishly climbed back into the cabin.

Paul seemed to be particularly pissed off. We needed a little extra help from our bag of tricks. I took a letter from our goody bag. It was from Bevan Cantrell, one of Paul's best friends, written before we came out, before Bevan lost his mother. The letter was so encouraging for Paul – Bevan was so behind him, said he really believed he could achieve what he aimed for. It was amazing what a little support could do to boost the psyche. I was delighted with my choice of letter. I rewarded Paul for his better mood with a picture from the goody bag of his dog Rhapsey, who died about a million years ago. Sometimes I look at Paul and he has the face and mannerisms of a seven-year-old boy. Giving him this picture was like offering him a symbol of comfort, like giving a small child his favourite stuffed animal.

Reflecting on Bevan's letter really brought home to us how important our families and friends were to us, and where our priorities in life lay.

Three days later, we were still on sea anchor. I was starting to get paranoid. In the night I thought our "sea-me" radar target enhancer was going to explode and that we were right in the middle of a shipping lane. This beacon picked up any ship's radar in our vicinity and sent out a signal that made us look much bigger on their screens than we were. These ships were massive and could run us down in the middle of the night without knowing it. When we were anchored, we were not on deck regularly at night with an eye open for the lights of a tanker.

I had high hopes that morning that we might get going again, but no joy! Paul rang the support boat to find out if there was any news, and they said it was going to be another 48 hours – disaster! I was absolutely disgusted at this. I felt like I was in solitary confinement. Every day was a little more discouraging. Our goal to reach Antigua in 60 days seemed to get further and further away every day.

I supposed we were going to just have to face the reality that we were trapped in this cabin. I felt so lazy, I had to do something. Hangman! The best time-waster in the world. Uh, I didn't seem to be as successful as I was last time. I moved on to Connect Four, but 20 minutes later I was bored of this, too. We listened to music, slept and ate. I decided to make a game out of eating our Twix bars. We got one stick each. The "How hard is it to torture Paul?" game was born. Paul usually hoovers his Twix bars down, leaving not even the crumbs, whereas I bite the sides first then take the caramel off, leaving only the biscuit. Paul looked like a starving puppy. No fear, his puppy eyes did not influence me at all. I usually took another ten minutes just to eat the biscuit, savouring every single bit. Paul was exhausted and hungry. But he knew he could not have another Twix for a day because we had to ration them.

I was thinking a lot about food these days. I sniffed. "Paul can you smell that?" Paul stuck his nose in the air, his nostrils doing their best to pick up the scent. "I can't smell anything," he said. "What is it?" I could smell roast chicken. I grabbed the binoculars and scanned the horizon. Perhaps we were downwind of a ship. We looked and looked but there was no ship. No roast chicken for me tonight!

I sat drawing all the amazing bits of food I missed. Sometimes I convinced myself I could even taste it, as though it had jumped off the page and into my mouth. And the aroma was so strong. Oh, I would have given my left arm to have the roast chicken I had just drawn. French fries, baked bread, pepper sausages from Tesco, stuffed potato with sour cream and bacon bits, ice cream – and my favourite of all, peanut butter, yummy in my tummy. This was like a scene out of *Peter Pan*, when the kids imagine their food and it comes true. I was on the verge of having an imaginary feast. "Starting to really question my sanity," I wrote in my diary.

Paul had found a packet of cards with pictures of Venice on them. This time last year we were there. What an amazing city! After playing "Shithead" and other card games for a while, I daydreamed for a few hours about the amazing places I had been. I had never stopped to acknowledge just how lucky I was to lead the life I did. As I was deep in this moment of reflection, Paul kept the mood light by plotting our position. He is such a numbers man. Every day he came up with these random figures. We were the epitome of man and woman. I lay daydreaming, and he played with numbers – chalk and cheese, we are. If we got a decent run with the weather, we might hit the halfway mark in 20 days. We needed to average 90 kilometres (50 nautical miles) a day, which I knew we could do. Overall, if the weather held, we could be looking at around 65 to 70 days. If the weather didn't hold, I didn't want to even contemplate how long it could take.

Today was a double birthday: our friend Miriam Walsh and my brother, Clayton. I could not wait to call them. When we got through, the reception was very bad. I hoped they knew we were thinking of them. There was a level of guilt on the row when you felt you were not there for people.

The next day, Monday, we were still anchored and the conditions seemed to be doing anything but lightening up. That morning, we saw our first ship, about 8 kilometres (4 nautical miles) away. It appeared to be a big tanker. Paul tried to make radio contact, but there was no response. I rang the support boat and gave them our estimate of the ship's course, in case it was heading for some of the other boats.

After all the excitement of actually seeing something, we cooked dinner and dumped our leftover food (no wrappers) overboard. A shoal of maybe 20 fish gathered around the boat. Some of them looked like mini-sharks, and a few were about 65 centimetres (2 feet) long, with silver and green reflective bodies and yellow tails. Unfortunately, I knew nothing about identifying fish. I supposed these could be yellow tails! We fed them, virtually hand-to-mouth. Paul thought about going swimming and then remembered a story Mick Dawson, one of the organizers, had told him about dusk, sharks and feeding. This did not sound like a good combination, so we decided bed was a better option.

We were now three weeks into the row and approximately two weeks behind schedule if we were to reach Antigua in 60 days. We had lost 90 kilometres (50 nautical miles) over the past few days, even with the sea anchor out. We had three texts that morning telling us we were going the wrong way. Thanks for pointing it out, guys. As if I didn't know. This was heartbreaking and truly testing my resolve. Each day we were anchored got me down but fired me up to reach Antigua as quickly as we could. The support boat informed us the first boat in the fleet got moving around midnight. Some of the boats fell one side of a line, and were out of the worst of the weather – the others, including us, were still stuck. Lin reckoned between midnight that night and noon the next day it would turn for us. We hoped she was right this time.

Paul and I had been discussing life after the row over the last few days. I was using the wonderful life I had had and hope to have to drive me on through these difficult times.

CHAPTER 20
Christmas on the High Seas

Paul ···

DAY 23, DECEMBER 22, 2005

I stuck my head out the cabin door shortly before 9 a.m. on Wednesday, December 22, praying that conditions might finally have changed. We were in luck. The wind was northwesterly, pushing us to the southeast – not ideal but good enough to get back in the saddle. I climbed out of the cabin for a closer look. Yip, we could give it a lash. I shouted to Tori: "Pup, I reckon it's good enough to get going again." We were both deliriously happy. The usual game of tug-of-war ensued with the sea anchor, but this time I was not that fussed. After six long days, we could finally get going again.

The night before had been a sleepless one, but by choice. We took it in turns to get up every two hours to check if the conditions had changed. When they did, even though we were a bit tired, we got straight back into it again. I knew our first series of night shifts would be hard, and I was right. This time I got through my shifts – but not without a scare. It was a dark night, but at around 3 a.m. I saw what I thought was light shining from a huge, dark shape on the horizon. For a few minutes I was convinced it was a big ship. I was on the verge of going into the cabin to radio the large craft that was bearing down on us. I looked closer. The moon was emerging from a big cloud bank. When I realized what was going on, I had a little chuckle to myself. "Perhaps," I thought, "I'm starting to go mad."

The next day, I felt really weak all day, the weakest I had felt on the row so far. I couldn't stomach breakfast, so I had a cup of soup instead. We did a few interviews that day: with Ed Myers on Live 95 FM and Tom McSweeney for *Seascapes* on RTE. Our pieces in *The Irish Times* were sparking interest, too. It was nice to know there was some support for us back in Ireland. The night shift was again a very difficult slog. I felt really down after my second shift, so I read Bevan Cantrell's inspirational letter again to give me a lift. And then, around 5 a.m., we saw our first whales. It gave us a boost, seeing the huge forms in the water. We peered through the darkness. We thought they looked like killer whales.

When I woke for my first shift of the next day, I hardly had the strength to lift my head, let alone go out and row for two hours in the blistering heat. Tori was shouting, "You're up in ten minutes." Dear God, no. I never felt so weak in all my life. A voice in my head began to speak to me: "Now's your chance, you asshole: you think you're tough – get up and prove it. Ah, poor little Paul is tired." I jumped up defiantly and banged my head hard off the cabin roof. "I'll show you," I murmured, as I started to see stars from the head bang. I often see stars if I get a hard knock in the head, probably as a result of knocking myself out off a goalpost when I was younger. Tori heard me talking to myself but just ignored it. We were both used to each other's little jolts of madness by now and took them in our stride. My energy burst disappeared fast, and as I began to row I felt weak again, like I was not in my own body. I think somebody had stolen mine while I slept and left me with an old woman's. So this is how Samson felt when he got the haircut! We had been a little sloppy with the consumption of our energy and electrolyte drinks, and it was starting to take its toll. I also needed to start eating more. Tori gave me a telling off for this. So for the whole day we both made sure that we were taking on more food, water and supplements and it seemed to work. We both started to feel stronger as night fell.

Christmas Eve was day 25 of the row – we had counted from November 30, nominating the race start day as day 1 – but something was wrong. We were in the middle of the Atlantic Ocean and it was virtually flat calm. It was like a becalmed lake, with no wind and soaring temperatures. The rowing was hard. I could feel the full weight of the boat with every stroke, as if I was pulling *Christina* from a standstill each time. "This is what the words 'hard slog' were invented for," I thought. But it was a good slog. It was honest; it was what the row was all about. We ground down the kilometres hour after hour, day after day. There was nothing fancy about it, but it was what would get us across. Sometimes I thought I could see Eamonn Kavanagh's face in front of me as I rowed, and I imagined him giving me the nod of approval as I punished my body day after day. Christmas Eve. Obviously you would think that it would not have felt like Christmas, but it did – for all the wrong reasons. I could not stop myself thinking about what everyone was doing at home and what I would be doing if I were there. I knew this was stupid, as it only tormented me. But I could not help myself.

We found a packet of olives and one more packet of peanuts that evening at the bottom of one of the hatches in the cabin. We felt like we had just won the lottery. Wow! What a feast we would have on Christmas Day. Tori chirped at me to open them, but I put my foot down: not until the following day. She laid it on thick, but I resisted her sales pitch. I actually hid them in a different hatch while she was rowing in case she got the munchies during the night. We decided to open some of the little presents our families and friends had given us for Christmas. One of the presents consisted of two Santa hats, some sweets and two mini-bottles of Baileys. We dragged the bottles in the sea to cool them. We felt like royalty as we opened a bottle of Baileys each with our dinner. "It's a pity we never recorded some Christmas music on the iPods," Tori said, mournfully. Cue my little surprise. I had 20 traditional Christmas carols on my iPod, and we blasted these out on our little stereo. We were happy and rowed well after dinner. Through the night we went, until 5 a.m., when we gave ourselves a little early Christmas present by taking two hours off.

We made a big thing of opening our Christmas presents now that the day had arrived. Mam and Dad had put in some more Santa hats, mini-whiskey and -Baileys, marshmallows, two hair clips for me (cheers, Mam!), some Christmas earrings for Tori and a little box of Pringles. The potato crisps were the present of our dreams. Both of us love savoury things, but we had not thought to pack crisps. Not a word was spoken for about ten minutes as we ate our way through the little box of Pringles as slowly as we could. We savoured the taste of sour cream and onion. I have a tendency to eat a little more quickly than Tori, so she monitored me, making sure I wasn't eating more than my share. There were 21 crisps, and neither of us was selfless enough to give the other the last Pringle. I suggested a game of rock, paper, scissors to settle the issue. Tori wouldn't hear of it; the stakes were far too high – a whole Pringle was on the line. So we split it in half and even poured the crumbs on to the lid to make sure these, too, were evenly divided. For a moment we were both four years old again.

We called our families, who were all in great form. My mother told me the priest spoke about us at midnight mass and also gave out our charity text line number for people to donate money. I got to say only a brief hello to Dad, which disappointed me. It's remarkable how we can take things for granted. Being at sea brought home to me how important family is and how much mine mean to me.

Tori and I took two hours off for Christmas dinner. We both ate our favourite rehydrated meal – pasta and cheese, and the bag of olives we had found. A friend, Egon Friederich, had given us a brack [an Irish cake or loaf containing seeds or fruit] he made himself, which he called sailors' bribe, and we toasted the last of it on our little gas stove and covered it in gorgeous honey. It was scrumptious!

We put the oars out and got back to work. Two things were causing me concern. Although the still weather made for a pleasant Christmas, at the back of my mind I was worried that this was the calm before the storm. My other worry concerned my nether regions. As the rowing seat slid forward and back, my two "family jewels" were getting caught, snipped so to speak, and they and their little home were being ripped to pieces. The pain was excruciating. Each shift was turning into a test of how much pain I could endure. Every two seconds I would grit my teeth, breathe in, and grimace with pain. I genuinely didn't know how much more of this I could take. I was about to get a late Christmas present from Tori. Shortly after midnight she heard one of my shouts of pain. The light went on in the cabin, and I could hear her rummaging. She opened the hatch and threw one of her thongs at me. 'Try this,' she shouted. I was willing to try anything. Feeling a little odd, I put the thong on and sat down. Oh, my God, I'm cured! I couldn't believe it – the pain went away immediately. The thong had lifted everything out of the way. No more catching, no more agony. I let out a roar and told Tori we'd be in Antigua when she woke up. The thong looked so wrong on me, but I didn't care, it worked. I was no longer suffering. Tori insisted on taking a picture, but it's safe to say it won't be appearing in this book.

Tori's problem solving continued through to December 26. She figured out a new stroke for calm conditions. If we dipped only half the blade of the oar in the water and pulled as if we were trying to put topspin on the water, our speed increased. I have no idea if this is a type of rowing technique, but it worked for us. Perhaps it was a reflection of how inexperienced we were. We both had a good laugh at the fact that here we were in the middle of the Atlantic in a rowing boat learning to row!

Our levity did not last. The calm appearance of the ocean started to disappear. At first it was hardly noticeable, just a slight increase in the wind, but the swell built up, and before long we were being thrown around by a giant swell of 12–15 metres (40–50 feet). For the first time, too, the waves were breaking in on top of us. The ocean's demeanour had changed; she was becoming angry and violent. I had a bad feeling things were going to get very ugly. Mother Nature was about to unleash one of her daughters, tropical storm Zeta. We were entering a monstrous washing machine – and not all the boats in the race would make it out in one piece.

CHAPTER 21
Gearóid and Ciaran Go Down

Tori ···

DAY 40, JANUARY 8, 2006

I totally lost the plot. I stood up in the middle of my shift and screamed at the oars in frustration at our lack of progress and our inadequate rowing technique. At that moment it seemed like our oars were almost slowing us down; each time we put them in the water it almost brought the boat to a standstill. I decided we should change the set-up of our rowing gears: if we rowed with our hands closer together our oars should have a longer stride in the water. I set out to do this, but I could not find the screwdriver. My coping skills failed me and some of my most unpleasant traits broke free – I looked something like Medusa. I did not save myself: I could only blame myself for not putting the screwdriver back where it belonged. This little bit of anal retentiveness came from my childhood. My dad would go mad if we did not keep his workshop clean. If we misplaced his tools, there would be hell to pay. "If you do not respect the area you live and work in, it is a reflection of not respecting yourself," he would say. Laziness was a very unattractive quality. Dad was a wise man, and I take his words and ways of life seriously. I was pissed off with myself for my laziness and for my failure to grasp how important these tools were to us. If we lost them, we were screwed.

I wondered if the world was against Paul and me. I asked myself why nothing was going our way, why we were always the unlucky ones. In this moment of self-pity, I had the nerve to say out loud: "I wish I was Gearóid and Ciaran, it seems like everything just happens easily for them."

The satellite phone rang. Getting through to our phone depended on sheer luck of the draw, so I was delighted to talk to someone. Paul's father, Bert, frantically asked how I was. Fine. Could he talk to Paul? Sure. This seemed a bit unusual but not seriously worrying. The line was bad, and all Paul got out of his parents was a frantic "Are you OK?" I joked, "Think your parents are really taking the row hard."

Five minutes later the phone started beeping like crazy. Six text messages in a row. Gearóid and Ciaran had set off their EPIRB! The EPIRB is the equivalent of an SOS; it should only be set off if something goes seriously wrong. This moment was surreal. Could I be reading this right? A million questions raced through my mind. I was almost scared to say them out loud to Paul for fear of hearing my own voice rehearse the awful possibilities. I did not want to believe this could actually happen to someone we knew. I was imagining the fear they must have been facing. Were they lost? Would anyone find them? What happened?

We called Lin Parker on the support boat and Paul asked her what was going on. "I do not know, I honestly have no clue." It was the most terrifying thing we had ever heard. The distress signal was picked up at around six o'clock. The support people had tried to ring the satellite phone and there was no response. The support boat was about ten hours away and was headed full tilt to the location indicated by the EPIRB. They asked us to notify them of any details we heard from the Irish media. How could we know more details than them?! Anxiety churned in my stomach as I realized that this was really happening. Gearóid and Ciaran were in a life-threatening position and there was nothing we could do to help them.

Our friends Daragh and Miriam called to tell us that the US Coast Guard had sent a boat and helicopter to the site of the distress signal and that there was a merchant ship about two hours from the site. I am not religious and I had never prayed before in my life, but now I addressed a few words to all the gods on behalf of the boys and their families.

We prepared for our night shifts around 8 p.m. I peered out of the cabin into the falling darkness. The ocean had a mission tonight. There was fire in her belly, fire upon the horizon as the sun set. In that moment, I truly comprehended the saying "at nature's mercy." I closed the door and muttered, "Please show the lads mercy." I could not imagine being in the middle of the Atlantic in the water at nighttime. It was probably my biggest fear, especially on a wild night like tonight.

Paul braved the night first. The rain had a cutting edge as it drove into his eyes. I know he was uneasy after the news we had got and was trying not to show any fear, to keep me calm. I could not sleep, fearing something might happen to us too. For the first time, I was fully conscious of the consequences of my decision to go in this race. Curled up in the little cabin, I imagined the terror the Lewis and Towey families must be feeling, and all the other families too. I felt so guilty for putting people through this. Anger boiled in my stomach. This was not fair! Gearóid and Ciaran did not deserve this. After all, we were the ones who had no business being out here; we did not even know how to row. Life can be so unfair. After facing the elements for an hour, Paul could no longer see the compass. With racing thoughts of the lads' disaster, he decided to come into the cabin and steer. We would put our safety first. Neither of us was going to row that night.

At 11 p.m. the phone beeped. Gearóid and Ciaran had been rescued by a Spanish tanker and were alive and OK. They would arrive into Spain in five days. Their boat was hit by a rogue wave and the cabin was ripped off. They were fortunate to make it into the life raft but had to cut the link to their boat, the *Atlantic Challenge*, in the dangerous conditions.

Now that I knew they were OK, my reaction was one of sadness that their row had ended like this. It must have been heartbreaking. It was just bad luck to be hit by a rogue wave; it could hit any boat in the race at any time. They were in the wrong place at the wrong time. It was so unfair. I was sure they were not thinking of it right now – they were probably just happy to be alive – but they had dedicated so much time and energy to this race, and I was disappointed it had to end like this for them. If this happened to us, I did not know how I would feel.

The following morning, I bought minutes for our phone to make sure we could contact our families at any time. We had made around 65 kilometres (35 nautical miles) the previous day, even though we only rowed from 9 a.m. to 11 p.m. That night, we would get back to our regular routine. As tragic as the event with the lads was, we had to stay focused because the reality was we were still out there. The sooner we got across the better.

Paul's parents rang that morning. Apparently the lads were front-page news at home and on all the television and radio stations. There had been a lot of talk about us as a result. Paul's dad had been fielding calls about us, and the media wanted to talk to us: Sky News, RTÉ Radio One, the *Limerick Leader*, the *Irish Examiner*, the *Irish Independent*. It seemed wrong that we might end up getting more publicity due to Gearóid and Ciaran's misfortune. It was sort of sad, not right, really. I guess, as my mom would say, that's life. We just had to get on with it.

I felt poorly motivated as we moved into the following days. I was having the worst acid reflux. Paul could digest rocks if he tried, and I felt so jealous. It was a simple luxury in life, but all I wanted to do was have a shit. I felt food come up but it would not go down. I hoped to get a hold of the doctor soon to sort this out.

Because of the wind and swell, we were in danger of getting too far south too soon. We were at around 18 degrees 30 minutes north of the equator and Antigua was at 17 degrees. I spoke to Eamonn Kavanagh to double-check this, and he told us to just go with the conditions, that the weather would push us to the west at some stage. Dan Byles on the support boat had the same message. Dan did the 1997 race with his mother, Jan Meek, and was a really nice guy. We followed the advice, but the hard part was that we were not taking kilometres off the distance, as the crow flies, to Antigua. We rowed a whole day and looked at the GPS and it showed that we were only 18.5 kilometres (10 nautical miles) closer to Antigua even though we had covered about 75 kilometres (40 nautical miles). I just wanted to scream!

My Auntie Peggy called. She had truly been a rock for me, my biggest fan. I wanted to pull through this to be a positive role model for my younger cousin, Chaim, Peggy's son. I thought about them a lot. Peg told us that Chris Martin, one of the solo rowers, had capsized in the last few days. His boat did not self-right because he was drinking his water ballast and had not replaced it. Fair play to him, though, he managed to right the boat himself from the water. He also lost his oars and hoped the support boat would replace them. Things seemed to be getting a bit more dangerous out here. Maybe we were all getting a bit complacent as we got more tired. We needed to keep our guard up and our minds sharp. Apparently, most of the teams had effectively stopped racing and just wanted to get to Antigua safely. Some teams were on sea anchor at night, preferring not to row in the rough conditions tropical storm Zeta was creating. I found Peg's words comforting, knowing that other people were experiencing the same emotions as us.

I was concerned about the position of our life raft, due to recent events. We'd had to put it in the bottom of the bow cabin because that was the only place it would fit. A lot of other boats put their life raft in their well for easy access, but in our boat, which was slightly different from the others, it was a tight fit. Realistically, I was not confident we would be able to get it out in time in case of an emergency. I was concerned that if the boat capsized and did not self-right, the hatch we needed to open would be submerged. Would the water pressure stop us from opening the hatch? Who do I always call on in time of doubt? My dad.

Dad is a hydraulics specialist and has a great knowledge of water pressure. He was so smart he grasped the point immediately. When I told him the size of the hatch and how deep it was, he was off: it would be three squared this and the square of that. Blah, blah, blah was all I heard, but somehow he came up with the answer. "Yeah, you would have about 20 seconds or so." In reality, getting the life raft out this quickly would be virtually impossible. "The best life raft you will ever have is your boat," he said. "Hold onto your boat as long as you can. Even if it is upside down it will still float." I love the way Dad has such great common sense. He always sees the obvious, which I do not, and that is why I always call on him.

Paul ··

DAY 43, JANUARY 11, 2006

"Success is not final, failure is not fatal: it is the courage to continue that counts." Winston Churchill's words had become hugely relevant to us. On day 43, January 11, with over two-thirds of our target of 60 days gone, we had nearly 3,000 kilometres (1,600 nautical miles) to go. And we were being pushed too far south by the weather. At this rate we might end up in Barbados – or Venezuela!

We decided not to row that night, as it would only accelerate our movement to the south. As we got farther west, the winds were supposed to push us more to the west, allowing us to make up ground to the north if needed. But so far on this trip, the Atlantic had done nothing it was "supposed" to do. There was no need to start panicking just yet, but we did need to keep a very close eye on our latitude.

Even as we struggled, Tori and I talked easily about what we would do after the row. Due to visa issues and decisions on where to go to college, Tori would have to return to Canada when we got back to Ireland, so we would be forced to do the "long distance thing" for a while. We owed too much money for me to join her there – trying to repay a large euro loan while earning Canadian dollars would not work. We decided to try to meet up in New York every few months, as it is halfway between Vancouver and Dublin. It is also a fantastic city and one that Tori had never seen. It was amazing how much looking forward to what we would do after the row helped to cheer us up and focus our minds on the task at hand.

As we went into Friday, January 13, the conditions, already bad, got worse. The swell was not huge, but it was very choppy and the waves were all over the place, making it difficult to catch the blade of the oar in the water. Every stroke was a battle against the conditions. My spirits were quickly dropping, and I was desperately trying everything I could to fight this. I did not want Tori to see any signs of my becoming disheartened in case it brought her down. I needed to be strong, and Friday the thirteenth was no time to start showing weakness. It was amazing how superstitious we became in this situation, and I understood why sailors tended to be like this. We were so reliant on Mother Nature – if she wanted to, she could finish us. Ordinarily I wouldn't be superstitious at all, but we were in a very vulnerable position and it played heavily on my mind every day.

Tori got knocked around a bit on her 2–4 a.m. shift and was quite scared when she finished. To make matters worse, the iPod took a knock and stopped working, so my 4–6 a.m. shift was songless. How powerful music is! Time appeared to go backward as I rowed with no musical stimulation. During the night it rained quite a bit, and with wet shorts the chafing got more painful. Being woken up at 3:45 a.m., exhausted and sore, to get into wet, salty shorts and row for two hours is not fun.

I was finding it very difficult to control my emotions; I felt like a madman some of the time, seeing only the bad aspects of things. On the evening of Saturday, January 14, I fished out a letter from our goody bag. It was from a friend of mine, Philip Duggan. Life is transient, he said, and in 50 years' time these couple of months would seem like a very short spell in the grand scheme of things. I took heart from this. He quoted Harriet Beecher Stowe, the American author and philanthropist who wrote *Uncle Tom's Cabin*: "When you get into a tight place and everything goes against you, till it seems as though you could not hold on a minute longer, never give up then, for that is just the place and time when the tide will turn."

I felt like we were in this tight place, and I really took heart from these words.

I am somebody who can be inspired and to me the source of the words, music or whatever it may be is irrelevant: it's the effect it has that is important. And Philip's letter had the desired effect. I was back up again. But just as I began to feel better, the ocean started to go even crazier and the swell picked up even more. "She can read my mind," I thought. She sensed my better mood and cackled, "Oh, no you don't, I'll get you down again." The swell was violent and dangerous. Over the past 45 days we had become used to wild seas, but what we had thought were rough conditions at the beginning were nothing compared to what we were up against that night. We were in real danger of capsizing. As I rowed, my mind was racing. What would we do if we actually capsized? If it happened, we should self-right, but you never knew. If we did not self-right, I reckoned I could turn the boat over from the water, although it would be a very difficult task, and probably quite terrifying, especially in the dark. There would also be a very real danger of knocking myself out – such was the madness of the swell. I tried not to dwell on this too much, but I wanted to prepare myself so I would be mentally ready if the moment came.

The ocean threw us around like rag dolls. She was unsettled and angry; the swell was coming from all sides and breaking in on top of us. The boat rocked uncontrollably forward, back and side to side. It was virtually impossible to sleep when we were not rowing, as we were picked up again and again and thrown against the side of the cabin. The sleep deprivation was killing us, but we kept rowing. In the middle of the night, the boat got picked up by a wave from the side and I thought, "Oh, shit, this is it, we're going over." It happened so fast: the boat went right over on its side, threw me off my seat and, just as I expected my head to meet the ocean, by some miracle *Christina* came back over and we avoided being capsized. We lived to fight another day.

The next day, I raided our emergency grab bag. We shouldn't touch it; it was for use only in the most dire need. But we had no more chocolate bars left in our stash, and we needed the pick-me-up. I reached in, found a mini-Mars bar and devoured it. Tori did her usual slow seduction of her bar and made it last for a good half an hour.

The ocean was angry again and we were both constantly wet, which made the chafing very painful. Tori was worse off than me – her bum looked like a pizza. She would not let the pain get to her; she truly has the heart of a lion. As the day went on, she kept getting belted around by the ocean. A gargantuan wave floored her and banged her injured ribs. She burst out in tears. "Come into the cabin, I'll take over," I shouted. "No. No. If I don't row, we'll never get to Antigua," she screamed back. I always knew Tori was gutsy, but this really brought it home to me. She truly is the bravest person I know.

Before we left the Canaries, Peter Kavanagh told us courage had nothing to do with not being afraid; it was how you faced the fear that counted. Often when I was at the oars, I would ask the ocean to go easy on Tori and give me the worst of the weather. Unfortunately, the ocean wasn't in a listening mood. I felt so bad when I heard her being clattered around the deck by the unforgiving swell, knowing there was absolutely nothing I could do about it. I fervently hoped that I would be the one out rowing if we capsized. I would hate for Tori to be out there. I was not trying to be brave or chauvinistic, it was just, I think, the instinct to protect the ones we love.

We called Daragh and Miriam to cheer us up. They had been out late the night before celebrating a friend's thirtieth birthday and were recovering in bed watching TV. I asked Daragh if he had the sausages on. "Do you really want me to answer that?" he asked. God, how I wished I was there. A leisurely breakfast. A fry! Was I on drugs when I decided to do this?

Just when you thought things could not get any worse, they invariably did. The chafing became almost unbearable again. The inside of my thighs, my scrotum and the crack of my ass were in pieces. I have no intention of being vulgar here, but I was in so much pain it would be remiss of me not to mention it. Our mood was getting darker. We got news that two more boats were out of the race. The *Sun Latte* team from New Zealand, which endured shark attacks, a leaking boat and capsizing, were picked up on Monday, January 16. The *American Fire* team had also gone down. They were sleeping overnight and got flipped over in the large swell. One of their hatches was open and so the boat didn't self-right. We had got to know both of these crews in the Canaries, and they were very nice people. These two incidents further highlighted to us the need to be 100 per cent safe at all times. I think it also brought home to many people outside the race how dangerous this event really was.

We spoke to Eamonn Kavanagh, who was following the race very closely. He told us to make sure we kept all our hatches closed and maintained our water ballast at all times in case we capsized. He reassured us that *Christina* was solidly built and could withstand everything that was being thrown at her. He told us that the second half of the race would be easier and quicker. Eamonn's words of encouragement helped pick us up somewhat. That night we rowed blind; there was no moon, which meant no light to see the dangerous swell. By midnight, we decided that conditions were too dangerous, and given what had happened to other boats, we decided to batten down the hatches for the night. Although our bodies badly needed the rest, this was very disheartening. Our progress was not good, and at this rate we could be out here for a very long time. We still had not even crossed halfway. Morale was low.

Philip Duggan had quoted Mark Twain: "It's not the size of the dog in the fight, it's the size of the fight in the dog." There was plenty of fight in these two seadogs, but it felt like we were up against 20 dogs. We were suffering badly out here. We needed a break with the weather, and we needed it fast.

Peter, Eamonn, Paul and Tori

La Gomera

"Push through the pain, face the fear to Valhalla and back, you're a Viking!"

The sea anchor

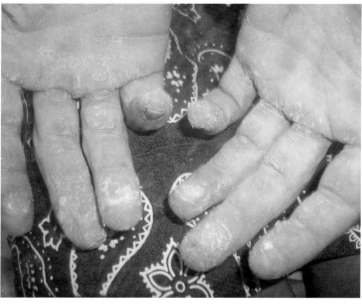

"Our hands often blistered as we rowed."

148

For most of the Atlantic crossing, Paul and Tori rowed naked. Sweaty, wet shorts can become encrusted with salt on an ocean row and lead to painful chafing.

Chilling our drinks in the ocean

Midnight snack

Making dinner

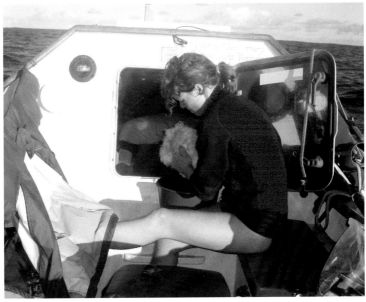

Cleaning our sheepskin seat covers

Barnacles underneath our boat

Scraping the barnacles

Christmas

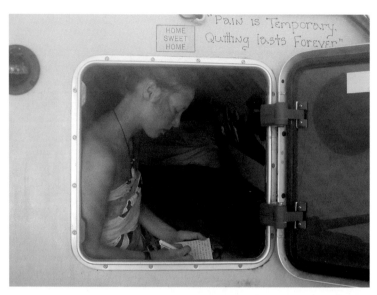

Dear diary

Deep in thought

"The weather was sultry, and we were both finding it very difficult to row."

Exhausted

"I was terrified, but I entered into the unknown again and started my night shift."

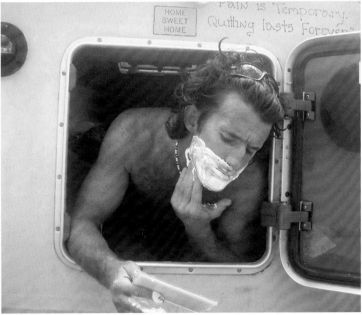

Bathing at the halfway point

With family in Antigua

CHAPTER 23

Barnacles

Tori ···

DAY 49, JANUARY 17, 2006

Halfway just did not seem to want to come, and I was at the end of my tether. It was day 49, January 17, and I seriously needed a pick-me-up. We had one present left on the boat, a weathered package from our friend Shane O'Neill, but there were strict instructions on it that it should not be opened until halfway. I sat in the cabin and looked at it. This was impossible! I usually knew what I was getting for Christmas about six months in advance; patiently waiting for a surprise was not my thing. It was driving me crazy not knowing what was in that package. As it was thrown around in the swaying cabin the tattered brown paper on the outside had started to rip. Paul was coming in soon, and I didn't want to get caught peeking, but I quickly peeled back a corner. There was a layer of bloody bubble wrap! I could not even feel what was inside and guess what it was. Was Shane trying to torture me?

Paul caught me fondling the package. With my puppy-dog eyes and best sales pitch I tried to convince him that we might actually die if we did not open this package. For 48 days Paul had stood between me and opening it. But everyone cracks sometime – and I found his weak spot. What if there were Taytos inside? And other treats? We had been fantasizing about new treats every hour of every day of the trip. His eyes lit up, and he grabbed the parcel and began to rip at it. The damn thing would not open! It was super-packed. He tore at it with violent intent. Everything in the package exploded into the air like a volcano erupting. It was like a dream come true: scattered around the cabin were five cigars and a lighter, a half-bottle of champagne, a book about the compass, a letter and 12 of the most delicious-looking chocolates I had ever seen. No Taytos, but Shane had come through. He was my best friend right then. Paul and I agreed we would have three chocolates each and save the rest for halfway. It was a reasonable compromise. After all, we did not want to have nothing to celebrate with if we ever got to halfway.

The elegant gold wrappers complemented the perfectly round chocolates. Had I ever seen such fine art? I carefully stripped off the outer layer. I wanted to savour every moment of this ecstasy, so I brought the chocolate to my mouth with great consideration as to how I was going to devour it. First I would just roll it in my mouth to make sure that every taste bud was evenly satisfied. I would then suck the juices out; then just let it melt. This could have been a seductive commercial, but I was not acting. There was not a word shared between us for the next 15 minutes as we finished all the chocolates we had allocated. Three each, all gone. We agreed that we deserved one more, just one more, no more than that. One went, two went, and . . . we had eaten them all. I was not thinking about the consequences of having no reward at halfway, as you cannot buy therapy as effective as this.

That day could have been devastating. After rowing seven hours we had only moved 19 kilometres (10 nautical miles). Producing results like this made it very difficult to go out and brave the wicked old night – to row my heart out when we could be sleeping and only go a kilometre. I had to ask myself why I was doing this, why even row at all? I could feel Paul's frustration. My negativity was bringing the team down. I needed to turn my head around and just face the night. I told myself that how you live your life depended on your perspective – it was up to me to fasten on the negative or positive end of the spectrum. I needed to choose the positive because it was not fair to Paul otherwise. Out into the sloppy conditions I went. The swell was of good size that night. Often two waves collided in front of me like two sea horses having a chest-to-chest shoving match. Sometimes there was a wave coming down in front of me: it was like a rugby tackle or an American football block. I decided to make this night a game to alter my negative perspective.

The ecstasy of the chocolate wore off over the next few days, a short, sweet interlude. The chafing on day 51 was unbelievably painful; I could barely sit down. If I was in the cabin I had to lie on my stomach to get any sleep. If the cheeks of my bum even touched the side walls of the cabin as the boat rocked from side to side I was awoken by a searing pain running down my backside. My ass looked red raw.

Just when I was feeling completely sorry for myself the satellite phone beeped. It was a message from Gearóid Towey. I was so excited: this was the first time we had heard from him since the capsize. His words were empowering, a reminder to appreciate all that we had. He was such an amazing guy – totally putting himself out there to help us. And he probably did not even want to think about the row after what had happened. "Enjoy every second out there," he said. "I know it's hard but it's very special; I am very proud of you both. Don't be in a hurry to use a drogue! Love, Gearóid."

It was amazing to think that after spending 24 hours a day with each other for over 50 days, we were still nattering away all day. That day's topics of conversation went from possible shark attacks to Down's syndrome babies to religion and grannies. We even called a friend of ours who was a doctor to find out the function of a thyroid. He must have really thought we were losing the plot.

We had no choice but to do everything in our power to keep ourselves preoccupied. These were the things that kept me going and passed the time. Otherwise we might have focused on more negative things. That day, water was leaking into the cabin from the hole where the wires from the solar panel came in. We had tried to shove a sock in there the night before, but the water seemed to get through no matter what we blocked the hole with. The next step was Sekaflex, a rubbery glue that would fill any hole. It's one of those must-have, can-fix-anything type of items. We hoped it would do the trick. There was nothing worse than lying in dampness; I just couldn't get away from this insanity.

It was heartbreaking on the oars that day: from 1 p.m. to 8:30 p.m. we covered only 13 kilometres (7 nautical miles). What the fuck was going on?! I was so frustrated. The boat was moving so slowly it would probably drift to Antigua quicker. I asked myself what was the point of even rowing. Thirty-three kilometres (18 nautical miles) today. It felt like someone was holding on to the back of the boat. All this was making me paranoid; surely we were not that bad at rowing, were we?

DAY 52, JANUARY 20, 2006

It all changed the next day. It was day 52, and we seemed to have found our big break. We discussed why we were going so slowly that morning and thought maybe it was the barnacles. While I was chucking the toilet contents over the side of the boat I decided to lean over a little farther and have a look at the bow. Oh, my God! There was an army of barnacles under the boat. They were hard to see because most of them were under the water line, but if I timed it so I was looking under when the waves rocked the boat back I could see thousands of them. Each of them must be at least an inch long. I checked both port (left) and starboard (right) sides of the boat before I informed Paul. Goose barnacles, he thought. He was not sure what to do about them.

He rang the support boat and spoke to Dan Byles. If we decided to get in the water and scrape them off, would we have to worry about sharks? There had already been two shark attacks in the race. Dan said the least of our worries was the sharks. The real danger was that the boat might smack one of us while we were in the water. He thought barnacles did not make a difference to speed – but everyone else on the support boat disagreed. Then he told us it took him over 100 days to row this ocean.

It looked like we were going to scrape off the barnacles and take our chances. Even though Dan had reassured us there was no danger of sharks, I could not help but hear the theme from *Jaws* in my head. I quickly decided that someone would need to stay on deck and play the lifeguard from *Baywatch* on the lookout for sharks (OK, I was too scared to go in the water).

Paul suited up in a fine fluorescent orange survival suit, as we suspected he would be in the water for a few hours. Just in case the sharks did not see him, the suit made him look like a life-size human fish hook. The suit was Eamonn Kavanagh's and was about three sizes too big, so if a shark got a hold of it, it would mostly be chomping on orange plastic. I should be able to rescue Paul before any real flesh damage had been done.

He had his goggles and snorkel on, and I had put Vaseline around his beard to try and stop the water from getting in. He had a scraper around his wrist, a knife around his leg and a camera in the other hand. Paul would be a tourist to the very end. Into the water he jumped. Even with the survival suit on, his eyes almost popped out of his head as the shock of the water hit him. Down he went! The entire bottom of the boat was covered with barnacles. As he scraped them off I moved the clip of his harness to the next grab line. Each time a wave smacked the side of the boat I cringed and prayed it would not knock Paul out. He had assured me the waves would do him no damage – his noggin had taken a few knocks in rugby and remained intact.

I looked out at the sea and realized there were the most amazing fish around the boat. They had come to the surface to feed on the floating barnacles Paul had scraped off. There was one little fish in particular, about the size of my hand with zebra stripes all down its back. I had never seen anything so beautiful in my life! If I were a fish this would definitely be the one I would want to be. I knew I should not tug on the harness unless I had spotted a shark, but I would have hated for Paul to miss seeing this fish, as it had been quite a while since our last marine spotting. I gave a little tug. Paul flew out of the water like a streak of lightning and hit the deck with a thud. "Where's the shark? Where's the shark, Tori?!" He looked so scared I thought he might have left his heart in the water. I sheepishly realized the consequence of my actions. I pointed down to the tiny little fish. My face was pink. "Isn't she pretty, though?" I think Paul was about to strangle me. His evil eyes pierced through me. "There were a lot of pretty fish under the boat, thanks. Only pull on the rope if you see a shark!" He was so shaken up he had to take a break and calm down. I think he was expecting to see a giant black fin heading straight for us. After ten minutes, he went back in the water. He worked for the next two hours, until the boat was virtually naked of barnacles.

I was first up to row. I could not believe it – the boat felt about 50 kilograms lighter. She was at home in the ocean again; she glided like a fish through the waves. The feeling was amazing, like someone had taken off our shackles or cut free an imaginary anchor. Free at last! All I wanted to do was row, row and row. I screamed out loud: "Thank God. It was not us, we do know how to row, we don't suck. Yeah! We might actually get there this year!"

CHAPTER 24
Halfway and a Third Person on the Boat

Tori ....

Our spirits were running high. Only one day after the discovery of the barnacles and we got to dinner on good mileage. We had rowed 15 kilometres (8 nautical miles) in four hours. The day before we rowed for eight hours and only made 13 kilometres (7 nautical miles). What an unbelievable difference! For the first time in the whole trip, I actually wanted to do a night shift. There was positivity on board that day, a feeling that we were going to really get to Antigua sooner rather than later. A rebirth of hope.

My usual nerves before starting a night shift were lying dormant. Somehow it felt right tonight. Paul had tucked himself into the *leaba* nicely. After about 20 minutes, the sun had left me and there was not a peep of light anywhere. The night was calm, although I would still have preferred to be able to brighten the darkness with a few stars. I felt like someone needed to open the closet door just a little to let a small glow of light in. Moonlight or starlight was like a small comfort blanket.

Around 8:30 p.m. the atmosphere started to change and the intuition that lay deep in my stomach started to grumble. It was stronger than I had ever felt it before. I wondered if I had eaten something to upset me. Suddenly I was scared. I remembered this feeling as a child after watching a TV show that scared me. I would always have to watch a happy show afterward to steer my imagination in the right direction. Otherwise I would go through the stages of being scared, starting out with the fun one, moving on to the nervous one and then to the genuinely "I am scared" one. This was not a good place to be, because there was no turning back.

As I sat there alone, I felt a cold breeze shoot up the left side of my neck. I found this very strange because there was little wind tonight, only a slight warm breeze hitting the right side of my neck. I stopped for a moment and tried to refocus myself and continue rowing. Then every hair on my body from head to toe stood up. I didn't know why, but I had a feeling that I was being violated. I was very uncomfortable with it. My natural defence system started to kick into overdrive, warning me of danger. "What's going on?" I asked myself; there could not be any danger on a calm night like tonight in the middle of the Atlantic. I felt scared to turn my head to the left. It felt as though there was a man standing right beside my face. Not a centimetre, an inch nor a foot away but literally right beside the left part of my face. He was so close I could almost feel him breathing on me. I told myself this was probably my mind playing tricks on me due to the sleep deprivation; all I had to do was to think about something else and it would go away.

I stopped for a moment to change my music. Goodbye Coldplay, hello to Madonna's more upbeat tone. The song starts. "Time goes slowly; time goes slowly . . . " Even though the tempo was upbeat, the words were cutting through me like a knife. The harder I tried to block out what I was feeling, the slower the time seemed to go. I just wanted to jump into the cabin and make this man go away. I did not understand why I felt so awkward and so uncomfortable. Why could I not shake this feeling? I could just turn my head to the left side; there would probably be nothing there. But this energy was so strong that I could not have borne it if I actually had seen something. I wondered if it was a ghost. Could it be harmful? When things like this happen, I mused, isn't it usually a comforting thing, like a guardian angel? But this was definitely not a guardian angel – all I felt was negative energy.

The only thing that took this stranger on our boat out of my mind was that I only had ten minutes left on my shift. When I finished, I frantically banged on the cabin, giving Paul the signal to get up. When the clock struck ten, I was in the cabin, my safe haven, so quickly I felt I had been saved from the bogeyman. I just wanted to get into my sleeping bag as quickly as I could and go to sleep to block this man out of my world. I did not say anything to Paul about my experience, as I didn't want him to think I was losing my mind.

Paul ···

"How was it?" I asked Tori as I struggled to get my damp shorts on while munching on an energy bar. "Okay, not bad," came the tired response. Same as usual. I harnessed myself onto the boat, climbed out of the cabin and began to row. The light was on in the cabin and I could see Tori climbing into her sleeping bag as I felt the pain of the first few strokes. These were always a bit uncomfortable, as it took a few minutes for our cramped hands to loosen up.

About 20 minutes into my shift, all of a sudden, out of nowhere, I got shivers all down my spine and pins and needles from my shoulders right down both arms. This seemed very bizarre to me, and I got a very unnerving feeling that somebody was standing right behind me, just over my left shoulder. I hesitated for a minute, wondering if I was going mad, before looking over my left shoulder to see if there was anything there. I nearly soiled myself: I saw the lower body of a man, from the hips down, dressed in a pair of black trousers and wearing black shoes. My heart skipped a beat; I turned away spooked and then looked back. It was gone. I was 100 per cent certain of what I saw. It was as real to me as this book you are now holding.

This mysterious shadow occupied my mind for the remainder of my shift. I wondered if this was the sleep deprivation, but I was sure of what I saw. After my shift, I climbed into the cabin, and Tori asked me how it was. When I told her what happened, her face went white as a ghost, and she told me about her earlier experience.

Tori

As Paul entered the cabin his face was deathly pale. I knew immediately he had met the strange man on board. Chills ran down my neck again as I found out that he even felt it in exactly the same place and had dared to look at it. My worst nightmare was confirmed. He actually saw it and it was a man. My intuition was right. I wondered if the sense of danger I was getting was correct as well. I was terrified, but I entered into the unknown again and started my night shift. Both Paul and I braved our shifts through the night feeling violated by the mysterious shadow on board.

Paul

I did not tell Tori, but my gut feeling about this mysterious shadow was ominous. Other boats had gone down, rowers had come close to dying; my first thought was that this black shadow was the grim reaper himself. Perhaps my time – or possibly our time – on this earth was up. After 54 days on the ocean, and having gone through some horrific and dangerous weather, this seemed a plausible possibility. Mother Nature might have been about to whip up another storm that would cost one of us our lives.

For the rest of the night, I contemplated my own mortality and thought about the possibility that I might be killed that night. My mind went wild; if one of us were to die out there I hoped it would be me. Obviously I did not want to die, but I didn't want anything bad to happen to Tori. She had too much to offer this world for her to die out here. I started to think about how Tori would cope with my death, and I found myself hoping she would get over it sooner rather than later and that she would go on to live a great and happy life. It was eerie to sit alone in a rowing boat in the middle of the ocean thinking that by the time the sun came up you might be gone. I worried about how my family would cope with my death. I felt so selfish for doing this row; if I died out here it would cause them so much pain.

Then my mood changed. This could not happen, I told myself. I shouted at the grim reaper to go fuck himself! I have an ocean to cross, you bollix. Piss off! You're not taking either of us!

When I joined Tori I did not share these thoughts with her in case they might freak her out. In fact I have not shared them with anybody until now.

Tori

As the sun rose, I felt my anxiety calm as the glow of light grew. The presence of the man became duller in the memory as the distractions of everyday life on board took over. At about 11 a.m., the most beautiful blue-nosed dolphin leapt out of the water right beside the boat. There was a pod of about seven of them. I thought for a moment the arcing dolphin was going to land on deck, it was so close to us. Their playfulness was calming; it was the same comforting feeling my dog would give me. I knew today would be a good day as they shared their cheerfulness with Paul and me.

The phone rang, always a huge highlight in the day. We figured that anyone who actually got through must have had the "force" with them. Ray Niland, a dear friend of Paul's, came on. I had never really talked to Ray in depth before, so naturally I assumed he would prefer to be passed over to Paul after a few short common courtesies were exchanged. I was pleasantly surprised by how genuinely encouraging and deep he was. I definitely underestimated this man. It never occurred to me that I had support from Paul's gang, outside my connection with Paul.

For a mid-afternoon snack I could only find the Swiss muesli, one of my most dreaded meals. It was a mushy mess when you put hot water on it. Out of laziness, I decided to eat it anyway and to slap in some cold water. To my delight it turned out that uncooked it was the best meal I had ever eaten. I felt like I had discovered the secret of life. These simple pleasures got me through the day: Ray and the Swiss muesli.

As the sun went down, the most amazing array of colours burst from the sky. The colour blue was the primary background, with bolts of fiery red exploding through it. Orange was there, too, and it was like they were having a battle, the orange as the neutral guy overwhelmed by the power of the red. Slowly the red took over, until the sky laid a blanket of fire above us. In my short life it was one of the most spectacular scenes I had ever witnessed. The day moved to night, with another brief encounter with the "shadow," and the night to day.

Over the coming days, Paul and I spent much time talking about the shadow and what or who it might have been. My grand-uncle, Jack Milburn, had been in the Canadian navy and would have been familiar with these waters. Perhaps it was him. Maybe he was here to keep an eye on us. Maybe this "shadow" was actually a good thing.

When I sensed the shadow again over the next few weeks, I spoke to it. "Okay, buddy, you're kind of invading my personal space here. Just back up, pick up the other set of oars and give me a hand here." He never helped us with the rowing but over the coming weeks I began to feel more at ease with this extra person.

DAY 55, JANUARY 23, 2006

We finally crossed halfway by 10 a.m. today – but we continued to row until noon before we celebrated. This was the most satisfying feeling of achievement, as there had been days when I really questioned whether we would ever get here. At midday, we opened the well-deserved half-bottle of champers and the cigars from Shane O'Neill. Two sips and I was three sheets to the wind; they say champagne goes straight to the head – and when you have been out at sea for over 50 days it shoots there a bit quicker. I lay in the cabin looking at the GPS and admiring our achievement. It said 2328 kilometres (1,257 nautical miles) to go and suddenly the goal seemed to be in sight.

We decided to reorganize the boat so that we could start the second half mentally prepared. We took all the food out of the hatches and created a mini-assembly line: we unpacked all the daypacks of food and sorted them into individual categories in each hatch. Seven hatches contained the seven flavours of meals – cod and potato in one hatch, chicken curry in another and so on. We were going to keep all bars and biscuits in the cabin for easier access. With the new space created in the centre of the boat we were able to move the garbage bags off the deck. All of a sudden there was an illusion of space. The boat felt like it had grown seven metres with a little scrub down.

To physically prepare ourselves for the second half, we each got to choose our own reward. I was up first and decided, after washing my shorts for the first time in a few weeks, to wash my hair. This would be the first time in 55 days. I had been keeping it back in a ponytail and had not even brushed it. My curly hair was wrapped around the elastic; they may actually have become one. Once I released it I hoped the hair would tumble free but it just stayed in position. It had been there for so long, it had turned into one big dreadlock, weaving itself around my head like a natural hat – it probably protected me from sunstroke.

I flipped my head upside down and dipped it into a bucket of lukewarm water. The water fought its way through the strands of my hair and finally reached my head. Ah! What a great feeling of cleanliness. I took about half a bottle of shampoo and massaged it into my scalp, releasing the oils. Slowly the hair started to relax. In my head, I was back on terra firma in a cool salon having my head massaged. My senses were heightened at sea and the wafting aroma from the shampoo seemed so strong I could almost taste the coconut. I lifted my head and Paul poured water over me until all the soap had entered the bucket. I looked at all the salt that had attached itself to my head like a parasite. I tried to brush out my dreads. Half an hour and a few balls of hair later, I was a new woman. My femininity had been renewed. My free-flowing, curly, strawberry-blonde hair blew in the wind, and I was ready to start the next phase of the trip.

Paul ⋯⋯⋯⋯⋯⋯⋯⋯⋯⋯⋯⋯⋯⋯⋯⋯⋯⋯⋯⋯⋯⋯⋯⋯⋯⋯⋯⋯⋯⋯⋯⋯⋯⋯⋯

My reward wasn't quite so soothing. I had decided some weeks before that when we crossed halfway, I would shave off my bushy beard. This was more a symbolic gesture than anything else. I had to clean myself up, lose the beard and refocus the mind for the second half of the trip. However, this proved to be a very painful experience. I discovered we had only two disposable razors on board. In the frantic few days before we set off, I had forgotten to buy some proper blades, which meant I must now tackle my facial hair with one slightly rusty disposable razor – Tori insisted I keep one for her to use on her legs and arms the day before we arrived in Antigua.

First of all, I hacked off as much of the beard as I could with a scissors. Then I began the painful process of scraping at the remainder with my increasingly blunt blade. Although this was very painful and took me an hour to finish, it had the desired effect, and once I had had a good wash I felt like a new man. Tori was gobsmacked by the weight loss shown on my gaunt face.

With the boat all tidied up, and Tori and me clean again, we were ready to face the second half of the trip.

Tori

I was the first to row, and Paul was sitting at the back of the boat. Everything was cleaned up and we were heading into good weather. All was well. We were both really proud, and this was the first moment I stopped to comprehend our accomplishment. We had actually rowed halfway across an ocean. Paul pulled our charts out, and in that moment as I glanced down at them I realized the depth and distance of 1,257 nautical miles rowed and had a moment of "Wow, this is brilliant!"

CHAPTER 25
Dear Dad

Tori ···

DAY 60, JANUARY 28, 2006

A few days into the second half and we were both exhausted. We had been making good speed and were pushing ourselves to new limits. This was day 60, the day on which we had thought we would finish. Like most things associated with this race, it hadn't worked out as we thought. The weather was sultry, and we were both finding it very difficult to row. The conditions were very calm, with no wind or swell. I was moving a dead body with each stroke; there was absolutely no momentum.

I had been thinking a lot about life these last few days. As the row stripped away the material needs, I realized that all that was important to me I already had – and probably took for granted. That afternoon I wrote Dad a letter. I was both inspired and surprised by how I was really leaning on the support of my family: my brother, Clayton; mother, Fran; father, Tom, and Auntie Peggy.

> Dear Dad,
> Just sitting literally in the middle of the ocean, somewhere between hell and back as you would say. It's not quite Valhalla but it will do. Have been reading your letter a lot lately. Every time I read it, it brings me to tears and the reason for that is because I think the world of you and always have. Your support and words of wisdom mean so much to me. I feel so fortunate to have had such amazing parents. I often think about when we travelled the United States in the sidecar of our Harley (not quite the usual family car) – how unique my childhood was, how innocent you guys allowed me to be for so long. I remember Circus-Circus in Reno (much better than Disneyland – a biker's Disneyland perhaps); [the motorcycle rally at] Sturgis (I was your sidekick and assistant photographer); all the KOA [Kampgrounds of America] campsites we stayed in (all the ice cream we could eat for

a dollar – how sick we got). None of my friends had the adventures I had at such a young age because of you guys. I loved the peanuts you used to bring from the plane when you came home from work [Dad works in a mine hundreds of kilometres north of home]. When you did arm curls with me and Clay I thought you were Hercules. Your loud music instilled the rebel in me, hopping across the floor to AC/DC. I was so proud when you built your Harley. It was the most beautiful bike I had ever seen in my life and I cannot wait for you to bring me to my wedding one day on the back of that bike. I love your nachos and sludge drink in the big cups. I loved always having the cool dad better known as "Captain Garlic." I love your big bad image (nine tattoos and a few Harleys). You had always been just a puddle of chocolate to me, always just my dad. I owe my happiness to you and Mom as you pushed me to be independent, outgoing, and you are the greatest example of an individual as you could ever find. I am so proud to be your little girl. I am still going to sit on your lap and kiss your forehead when you're all wrinkly in a wheelchair.

Just wanted to write you this letter to remind you, you are "forever my hero and forever my friend."

Love, your greasy little spider, Tor

I planned to get across this ocean so that I could give my dad this letter in person; I hoped it would be as valuable to him as his letter had been to me.

To my delight, the phone beeped. The text messages spurred us on. It was a local supporter from Arklow who'd sold us our satellite phone. The text said: "You are now officially the most experienced ocean rowers in Ireland, with Eamonn and Peter [Kavanagh] finishing in 58 days in 1997. From Egon [Friedrich]."

That was really what I was going for – not! The phone beeped again with some more uplifting facts. We had heard that the first few boats were home. "Another team has finished the race successfully – *Team*

Scandlines," read the text. I was very happy for *Scandlines*, but I could not help thinking that we had only crossed halfway a few days ago, and it was a little embarrassing to be so far behind. How I envied them at this moment. They were probably cracking open the champagne with all their family there to support them. What I was most jealous about was that they would be having a proper cooked meal with real food. Oh, I could taste it. I had to force myself to think of something else before I started to drool.

Rowing in dead heat and flat calm conditions can be torturous. We wanted to break through the 1,000-nautical-mile (1852-kilometre) point by the next day, and we decided to row together for the full day for the first time in the race. We started out rowing for three hours straight, averaging about 4.8 kilometres (2.6 nautical miles) per hour, which was not a bad speed but not a great speed with two people rowing. We were exhausted by 12 o'clock, and we stopped for a two-hour lunch break.

We ran the water-maker for the entire 120 minutes. With the smouldering heat, we kept running out of water by midday. It was so hot, any liquid I put into my mouth seemed to just pour out my pores. When you looked at the water, you could see it steaming off into the air. My head was faint, and all I wanted to do was jump in the deep blue sea. We were exhausted, but we had to keep going. We put mini-speakers on the deck. We cranked up Coldplay for 40 minutes to put us in the mood, then we moved on to Queen's "We Will Rock You" for a little push. With every beat of the song there was a stroke on the oars. On into "We Are the Champions." At the top of our lungs we sang to the open sky and the few small birds that surrounded us. They flew away. By the time our Queen selection came to an end, our speed had faded back. We swapped positions, with Paul moving to the stroke seat because we thought his weight in the bow position might have been lowering *Christina* in the water. We had to be careful at that moment, because the weight was distributed differently than when we left La Gomera. At around 4:30 p.m. we took our next break and adjusted the angle of my oars.

Paul decided it was time to take a dip and jumped head first into the unknown. I was more of a stay-in-the-boat kind of girl. Looking at Paul was torturous. I was so hot but could not bring myself to get in the water. There was not a ripple, and I could swear we were on a beach;

all we were missing was land. It was so hot Paul almost sizzled as he hit the water. His face turned from bright red to the natural pale shade of pink it should be. As he floated in the water, we realized just how quickly the currents were going. Within only two minutes the boat had passed him and he had to swim to keep up. Every time I turned my head, I thought I saw a fin out of the corner of my eye. I knew if anyone was going to get attacked by a shark it would definitely be Paul and me. After all, this was the man who got hit by not one but two cars on the cycle in Australia!

I was broiling. I decided to dip in one foot at a time. I attempted to dangle the two at once but could not hack it. Duh duh! Duh duh! The *Jaws* music playing in my head. I was going no farther. I knew what happened in those movies!

At 5 p.m. we resumed rowing. We rowed together until six, but our speeds were down to 4.3 kilometres (2.3 nautical miles) per hour, so we decided to revert to our one-person rowing shifts – we averaged about 3.2 kilometres (1.7 nautical miles) per hour alone, so teaming up was not worth it in our drive to break the 1,000-nautical-mile barrier. Going into our night shift, we knew we had a real battle if we were to hit our target. We were both exhausted because of the heat of the day and through my night shifts I could barely keep my eyes open. There was an amazing sky, really spectacular, and it seemed like I could see the whole galaxy. But I was too exhausted to really enjoy and appreciate what I was seeing.

As I rowed out of the night and into the daylight, Andrea Bocelli created the ideal atmosphere to accompany the perfect scene on the horizon. The sound of his voice warmed me internally; the calming but strong and confident sound projected into my ear and straight to my heart. All of a sudden my exhaustion lifted as I acknowledged the moment. I stopped and really appreciated how truly unique these experiences were. How many people had ever seen a proper sunrise, with no pollution? It was absolutely breathtaking. There was no fire in the sky today, no "shepherd's warning." It was going to be another excruciatingly hot day.

Paul burst from the cabin gasping for air. He did not take well to the heat and he was covered in sweat from head to toe. He stepped out of the cabin but was so weak from his exhaustion he could barely stand.

He tried to sit outside the cabin door, but the frame hurt his bony bum; he found a place at the bow but unfortunately his weight there dipped the bow lower in the water and made it very difficult for me to row. I asked him if he would mind returning to the stern. The thought of having to re-enter the cabin nearly killed him. He looked like a child deprived of his nap winding up for a temper tantrum. Maybe he'd throw himself overboard.

The phone beeped – thank God! It distracted Paul from his misery. Diarmuid, a friend of his, had left us some quotes to lighten the day. I wondered if there was a hidden camera somewhere because people seemed to know when to contact us. Paul sat down with the distraction of his toy and read: "Before you judge someone, you should walk a mile in their shoes. That way when you judge them, you are a mile away and you have their shoes." "If at first you do not succeed – do not skydive!" The next one brought a deep chuckle from me as I thought of my dad and how he would love it: "Give a man a fish, he will eat for a day. Teach a man to fish and he will sit in his boat all day and drink beer."

Thanks, Diarmuid. They got us through another day.

Paul ···

We hit our target. On day 62 of the row, our GPS showed only three digits – 999 nautical miles (1850 kilometres) to go. This was a massive milestone for us. We targeted hitting this figure on this day and we did it. We got a message from Gearóid Towey that morning: "Sometimes you eat the bear, sometimes the bear eats you. Eat the fucking bear!" Gags' words of encouragement meant a lot to us. Coming from somebody who had been out here and knew what it was like, his words carried more weight than most. I read the text out to Tori. Its effect was instant. Her face brightened up in a smile and she repeated the message quietly to herself several times as she rowed.

We were making good progress, but we had a difficult choice. The wind and swell were running south-southwest, and this could spell trouble for us. If we went with the prevailing conditions, we would be pushed farther south, so we would have to hope conditions would change to allow us to make our way back up north. This was what the wind and swell "should" do, but so far on this trip the Atlantic had done very little that it should or that it normally does, so we were understandably skeptical. The second option was to roll the sleeves up and cross the swell. This would mean much slower progress: days, perhaps weeks, of awkward and slightly dangerous rowing as we tried to climb our way back north. It wasn't an easy decision. The first course of action would be easier but my gut feeling was that we would have to take the road less travelled and cross the swell. We were 55 kilometres (30 nautical miles) south of Antigua already and I did not want to take the chance of getting pushed farther south.

We decided to call Eamonn Kavanagh to see what he thought. He confirmed that we were correct in the way we saw our options, but even with his wealth of experience he admitted it was not an easy choice. Tori and I discussed it and decided that it was time to stand up and fight; we would cross the swell. We had been hoping we would reach Antigua in three weeks; this decision would make that goal all but impossible to achieve. Although we knew we had made the right call, it was heartbreaking to know we could be going much faster if we changed our direction slightly.

We got another poignant text message, from Eugene Garrihy, later that day. We had never met him but he had been following the race very closely and had sent us many text messages of support. He quoted Mia Hamm, the legendary US soccer player: "The vision of a champion is bent over, drenched in sweat, at the point of exhaustion, when nobody else is looking."

We got some news that confirmed for us that the hard road was the right one: two teams had had to get a tow near Antigua. *Row4Life* and *Atlantic Warrior* had been pushed too far south and were in danger of being forced onto the rocks on the island of Guadeloupe, 55 kilometres (30 nautical miles) south of Antigua. The crews would be credited with rowing the Atlantic but disqualified from the race. It was very important to us that we finish under our own steam and reach Antigua no matter what it took. If that meant struggling across the swell, then so be it. We knew it would be worth it in the end.

Tori felt very ill after dinner and was getting sick as she rowed. She had eaten very little and was quite weak and weary. In typically defiant mode, she said she would row through it. I told her I didn't mind if she took some time off to recover, but she was having none of it. She really is the toughest person I know. As we rowed through the night she began to feel better. By morning, although we had only covered 65 kilometres (35 nautical miles), we had made 7.5 kilometres (four nautical miles) back to the north. Our fight back had begun.

The days that followed were hard. We averaged only about 65 kilometres a day, but it was our progress north that mattered. We made almost 20 kilometres (10 nautical miles) back in one day and were thrilled with ourselves. I remembered Eamonn's words when we rowed *Christina* from Arklow to Dublin and we had struggled against the tide. "That is what the Atlantic race will be all about," he said. "Plodding along day in day out, scraping for every mile for weeks and months." That was how we would get across, he said. He was right.

Day 66 proved to be one of our best. I spoke to my father, who told me that my sister Audrey might be able to make it out to the finish line. I really didn't expect this, as Audrey was living in Bahrain and had been home for Christmas. I just presumed she would not be able to get time off to make Antigua. I was so lucky to have such a loyal and supportive sister. Apparently she didn't ask for the time off, she told her employers this was a once-in-a-lifetime event and she was going. The news had lifted my spirits enormously. And there was more good news to follow; we got a text message from Tori's mother, Fran, and I couldn't stop smiling as I read it aloud: "Hi, guys, hope everything is going well. You're making great progress. Tori, your father has got an extra week off and we are looking at flights going out [to Antigua] on 19 February and coming back on 5 March." This nearly brought a tear to Tori's eye. I was so happy for her. Tori's dad is a heavy-duty mechanic in the diamond mines in the Arctic. He works two weeks on and two weeks off. He is flown up specially and the entire camp is on a strict rotation schedule – changing this is nearly impossible. We now had a time window to make Antigua.

Tori

Dad had been such a driving force for me during this trip; I would be so proud to arrive into Antigua and see him standing there. I knew I would feel so honoured to make him proud; it would be like living up to my mentor. I could not believe he just said to his boss that he had to come to Antigua. Apparently he walked into his boss's office and said his little girl was rowing across the Atlantic. "I will be there to see her." He said he would do it even if it meant having to quit. His boss agreed to give him the extra week off. Mom and Dad were trying to sell their house, and it was not that easy for them to just pick up and go. I had the most powerful driving force of all: love. Mom, Dad and my brother, Clay, really had been the fuel of my fire. I had not given up on myself in hard times, because they stood behind me and supported me.

Paul

We were on a mission. I checked the log and did the numbers. "If we can average 78 kilometres (42 nautical miles) a day, we can make Antigua by February 23." "Paul, we can definitely do that, I'm not accepting anything less," Tori came back, and grabbed the oars, throwing all of her 45-kilogram (seven-stone) frame behind each stroke. We both agreed that failure here was not an option – we would make Antigua by the 23rd. I would advise my family accordingly. The effect was instant: we had our best day so far, 81 kilometres (44 nautical miles) and we were only 7.4 kilometres (four nautical miles) south of Antigua. Although it remained quite difficult to cross the swell each day, we were fighting hard, and for now at least, we were winning the fight.

Conditions turned in our favour, with the swell below 5 metres, and Tori and I were both ripping out speeds of 5.6 kilometres (3 nautical miles) per hour. By day 69, the GPS showed 750 nautical miles (1389 kilometres) to go, another milestone. Better still, we were now back up to our desired latitude of 17 degrees. Our chafing was terrible, so we washed our sheepskin seat covers – Tori even sacrificed some of her nice hair conditioner to help soften them – and this eased the pain.

DAY 74, FEBRUARY 11, 2006

Just after lunch on Saturday, February 11, I spotted a boat on the horizon due east of us. I got on the radio and found it was the *Aurora*, one of the support boats for the race, and they were going to pay us a visit. We were so excited – for the first time in 73 days we would see another human being. Over the next 40 minutes, as they approached us, we pretended they were pirates and that we were trying to outrun them. In the excitement of it all, we completely forgot that we were both naked, and as they approached we had to scamper into the cabin to throw on some clothes. The *Aurora* came to within 100 metres of us, and we chatted to Lin Parker and Dan Byles over the hand-held radio. Most of the team were out on deck, and as we chatted I noticed one of the girls coming out of the cabin eating something out of a tin. I asked Lin what this was. A brief pause. "It's tinned oranges, Paul," she replied. We must have looked like Homer Simpson as our mouths opened, and we began to salivate. How good they must have tasted. Although we were not allowed to take anything from the support boat, I suggested to Lin that we wouldn't tell anyone if some tinned fruit or a beer happened to "accidentally" fall overboard. They were all out of beer, or so she said. I asked Dan, who rowed the Atlantic in 1997, whether the weather this time was normal. He laughed. Definitely not the norm. This was way worse than any other race. After half an hour of chatting, the *Aurora* left us. Our brush with humanity left us on a high.

Another day, another milestone. The day following our encounter with the *Aurora*, we broke through 500 nautical miles (926 kilometres). In a week and a half, we would see our families once again. I spoke to Mam and Dad; I could not wait to see them. Although I had spent the past few months thousands of kilometres away from them, in a strange way I felt much closer to them at this point. Given everything that had gone on, I appreciated my family much more. I realized that in the past I might have taken them for granted, and I was really looking forward to spending more time with them over the coming months.

That night, about 20 minutes into my first night shift, I got a strange and eerie sensation. Shivers ran up my spine and down my legs and arms. Could this be the "shadow" again? I felt like there was somebody behind me. I looked over my right shoulder – nothing. I checked over my left shoulder – nobody there. As I turned to face forward, I could see an arm coming in under my left armpit, mimicking my left-handed rowing action. I nearly shat myself. I looked over my left shoulder to see if there was anybody there. Nothing. Was I going mad? I would usually be quite skeptical about these sorts of things, but I definitely saw this. I decided to take it as a sign; at the time I was still crossing the swell to maintain our course. It was a little dangerous. Perhaps somebody was telling me to pull more on my left and straighten up. I straightened up the boat. I felt much more comfortable about this presence now. Who was it? I wondered. Was it really Jack Milburn, Tori's grand-uncle? "Jack, there's another set of oars there," I told him. He was having none of it, and I rowed alone for the rest of my shift.

By this point in the race, six crews had had to be rescued at sea after being capsized by the Atlantic swell. One of the boats, *Spirit of Cornwall*, went down with only 180 kilometres or so (100 nautical miles) to go. We needed to be on our toes for the next ten days. Hopefully we were now through the worst the weather could throw at us.

Tori ···

DAY 77, FEBRUARY 14, 2006

Today was Valentine's Day, and it was the first time in three years as a couple that Paul and I had spent this day in the same place. Not really the romantic setting I was hoping for, but we would work with it. During lunch, I made a card, since the Hallmark version was out of reach. I purloined five spare sheets of our journal because I love Paul, though I was worried we might now run out of paper.

In thick black marker, the first page asked: "Will you be my Valentine?" with a big throbbing heart. Second page: "I love you more than ice cream with cherries on top." He surely knew the seriousness of this call, as I would have given my left arm to have had this dessert. True love, indeed. Third page: "'Cause I think you're kind of hot, sizzle . . ." This was not just a figure of speech – the sweat dripped down his forehead as the heat rose in waves from the deck. Fourth page: " . . . plus, you're stuck on this rowing boat with me. If you will not be my Valentine, I'm not rowing." Oh, I had never felt so powerful. On the last page the soppy stuff: "Love always, your one and only pup." The love in the air pushed us on to achieve great things – we would do almost 100 kilometres that day!

The day rolled into night, and nighttimes were always a struggle. About four hours in, I could barely stay awake. The seas were calm, so there was no adrenaline, no fear challenging me. My head bobbed, and I held the oars tightly. My eyelids were heavy and I could barely peer out. Every few minutes I screamed to startle myself awake. I would have slapped my face, but I had to keep my hands on the oars. As I shook my head from side to side, I caught a glimpse of a light. At first I thought it was a shooting star, but I glanced over my shoulder for a second look. I saw a variety of lights – a navigation light and two others. Not a star; a big ship. The distance from the front to the back seemed enormous: could a boat really be this big? I banged on the cabin and woke Paul. "Holy shit! That tanker is really close to us," he said. Within seconds it had closed on us. It was really moving, and we had to react. These tankers were so big that they could run over us and not even notice; we were too small to even show up on their radar. We prayed that there was someone on night watch who would spot our helpless little rowing boat. Paul frantically turned on the radio and sent out a call: "To the vessel in approximate position N 17 degrees 10 minutes; W 55 degrees 22 minutes, this is the rowing vessel *Christina*. Come in. Over." We waited. I rowed as hard as I could in the opposite direction. Paul repeated his message. And repeated it again. I stood up and got our collision flares ready as the tanker closed. Finally, a response, in English. What sounded like a young Eastern European man came back in a friendly but lonely voice, telling us he was the second mate on the tanker. After a few moments he spotted us. We breathed a sigh of relief.

He was a young Bulgarian who sounded as if he too was struggling to stay awake this lonely night. He told Paul he was daydreaming about his fiancée, whose name was Christina, when he heard her name on the radio. He listened calmly for a second before almost falling out of his chair at the thought that he could be about to run down a small boat and daydream through it. He told us his vessel was 150 metres long with a gross displacement of over 18,000 tonnes. How big was our craft? We told him. He laughed. His ship had moved past us now, and we had to wrap up our little chat, as we were beginning to lose coverage on the short-range radio. "Do you mind if I ask you a personal question?" our passing friend asked Paul. "Fire away." Would Paul and I be getting married in Antigua? We said no, we'd just be drinking a few beers and enjoying meeting up with our friends and family. There was loads of time for marriage. "No, no, you never know what could happen, you should get married as soon as you can. Don't wait any longer." He seemed like a lovely guy. For five years he had been second mate on this tanker, making its way from the US to Sierra Leone in West Africa. Our friend said it was fine for him 20 metres above the ocean on his large tanker but that what we were doing was real seamanship. I felt like a proper seafarer after this encounter; it buoyed me up for my remaining night shift.

We were only about seven days from Antigua. The conditions were good, but we both felt restless and unmotivated. I hoped this week wouldn't seem to last forever, like the night before Christmas for a young child. We had both realized by now the truth of Eamonn Kavanagh's statement that this was primarily a mental challenge. Pushing through the misery at night, in particular, was a case of mind over matter. The only way to face the night shifts was escapism. My shift started by gripping the oars, one stroke, two strokes . . . by three strokes the mind started to go and the link between my eyes and brain disconnected. I was no longer looking at black sea but at the most vivid pictures. My desires in life came out to play. I usually started out with a chat. It might be with my best friend, Jeannine, or with my mom. We had a long conversation over a few glasses of wine. I usually got to a point in the show where I rewound, maybe changed my outfit or added a person, even down to a change in the smallest detail of the wall décor in the room. I manipulated the conversation. Then did it again. And again . . . to the point of obsessive compulsion. It was almost a form of meditation for me; it brought me to an inner place.

I also relied on the power of music. My favourites were Madonna, The Black Eyed Peas and a jazz mix. Madonna is my favourite singer, and her CD *Confessions on a Dance Floor*, worked well on the row because there were no breaks between her songs and it lasted just over an hour on my iPod. Psychologically it helped me to get over the halfway point in my two-hour shift. On CDs where there was a pause between the songs, I found myself counting the hour by how many songs I had listened to, which could drive me crazy. As I listened to Madonna, I pretended I was on stage or I was singing at a friend's wedding. Beverley Knight was another favourite. As her soulful voice ran through my ears, with every beat I took another stroke. I lost touch with reality, not even realizing that my eyes were closed and I was belting out the words of a song. Paul said he thought he heard wailing banshees at night. Every once in a while, I hit a note that was a little out of my range and Paul jumped from the cabin thinking I was screeching for help.

Paul sang as well. Not Madonna; more along the lines of old Irish ballads and rugby songs: "The Isle," "Fairytale of New York" and Christy Moore standards. They were like an Irish history lesson. I lay in bed and imagined an old man in a pub telling his story.

Paul ···

Music was powerful out there. On many a nightshift I really struggled before AC/DC or U2 kicked in and got me through the finish line. Out there, you clung on to whatever worked for you. We had a game where we imagined what famous actors would play our friends and family in a movie. Then we imagined what animals our friends resembled. These sorts of things got us through the long, difficult nights and helped us keep our sanity. I imagined things I wanted to do after the row; job interviews I would have, holidays I would take. I imagined these things in great detail, and they gave me something to look forward to other than my crappy two-hour disrupted sleep after I finished my shift. It was quite therapeutic. I had plenty of time to think about what I wanted to do after the row and what I wanted out of my life in general. I think that in normal, everyday life back on dry land, we are all too busy to take this time out to think about what we are doing, where we are going in life and whether we are 100 per cent happy with our lives.

Tori

I heard Paul talking to his father. He came into the cabin and I asked how his shift was. "Not bad, went to see a match with Dad. Munster won 22–17, just snuck it in the last few minutes. We decided to go for a few pints afterward. Mam wasn't too happy when we came home a bit wobbly." "Sounded like a great day," I said. "Tell your folks I said 'hi' next time." And out the door I went to start my next shift. It was an insane cycle, but it worked for us and it was getting us across an ocean. The power of the mind!

Paul ···

It was getting closer by the day. We had only about 450 kilometres (243 nautical miles) to go; we were making good progress, and on day 80 we were about to see one of the sights of the row. I was sitting at the oars, content after a big meal and happily looking around me, when I saw a huge sperm whale. It was only 50 metres away and getting closer. I yelled into the cabin for Tori to come and see. The massive creature changed course and began to glide across the swell in front of our eyes. It was a magnificent sight: about 10 metres (33 feet) long but not at all threatening. It moved lazily, as if it had not a care in the world, a gentle giant. Tori and I were buzzing – we had finally got to see something really special up close.

The very next day we spied a less welcome sea creature – a 2-metre (6½-foot) shark very close to the boat. Luckily, I had scraped the bottom of the boat for barnacles only a few days before. That was the last time I was doing that!

A Canadian freelance journalist who was in Antigua called us to interview Tori. This was the first real media interest from Canada. I thought it was disappointing that we got such widespread coverage in Ireland – weekly pieces in a main national newspaper, *The Irish Times*; slots on the Gerry Ryan show; spots on news bulletins – yet hardly a word had been written in Canada about Tori, who would soon, we hoped, become the youngest woman in history to row across an ocean.

We were suffering physically now. Both of us had pressure sores, and my lower back was sore and the skin on the sole of my left foot had cracked open. Worst of all, Tori's chafing was reaching new levels of agony. She could not sit down in the cabin when she wasn't rowing. She had fought heroically through much pain on this row, which constantly impressed me. But it did not surprise me. When we were preparing for the row, we had incorporated some indoor climbing into our gym sessions. I would climb a certain route and Tori would follow. Even as the climbs became harder, Tori would refuse to accept failing to climb anything I had climbed. By the top of one climb she had lost feeling and strength in her hands but she clung to the wall using her forearms. The instructor said he had never seen a more determined person on the climbing wall.

As we had rowed through the time zones, we had put our clock back, and on day 81 it went back a further hour. Another hour gained to row, we told ourselves. But we had started to slow down. We couldn't get above 3.7 kilometres (2 nautical miles) an hour. This was frustrating. The boat was free of barnacles and conditions were calm. However, during the day it was blisteringly hot. When I was not rowing, I either sat in the sweat box that was our cabin or stood outside the cabin in front of Tori as she rowed. Standing was the last thing I wanted to be doing when I was completely exhausted after two hours' rowing, but sitting at the bow dipped the boat slightly in the water and we didn't dare leave the cabin door open – it was unlikely in these conditions that we would capsize but we were not going to take any chances.

Antigua was so close, but this part of the trip seemed to be the hardest. I realized on Sunday, February 19 (day 82), that we were not going to make it to the end by the following Wednesday. Due to our recent good progress we had pulled our target back to that day. But now I could see that we would have to work really hard if we were going to make it in daylight on Thursday. What was another day, after over 80? Looking in from the outside this might seem a logical question. But for us an extra day at this stage felt like a week.

Things were bloody hard that Sunday night. By evening the swell had started to pick up and we knew we needed to row across it if we were to stay at the correct latitude. We hadn't enough water to drink because we had drunk too much in the sweltering heat of the day. We both collapsed at 1 a.m. Tori puked several times; I suspected a touch of heat exhaustion. We started again at 4 a.m. As morning arrived, I rang Dad to tell him that we wouldn't make Antigua till Thursday.

Within a few hours, we crossed W 57 degrees 37 minutes, the meridian of longitude deemed to be the other side of the Atlantic. On this Monday morning, February 20, we could claim to have traversed an ocean. I spoke to Niall Cantrell and his daughter, Keely, to let them know that we had now officially rowed across the Atlantic and to reiterate that it was in honour of Niall's wife, Lynda. With another

215 kilometres (116 nautical miles) to go, the milestone brought us little pleasure. We needed to maintain an average of 70 kilometres (38 nautical miles) each day if we were to hit Antigua in daylight hours on Thursday.

The ocean just wouldn't let up on us. Tori was in tears that we might not make Antigua on schedule. I was also very down; I did not want the row to finish on a low note. I called Lin Parker on the support boat, and she told me that most of the boats slowed down about 180 kilometres (97 nautical miles) out from Antigua, then picked up speed with about 130 kilometres (70 nautical miles) to go. She suspected we might be in some sort of back current. This lifted our spirits and gave us the little ray of hope we needed.

Now that we were on Antiguan time (four hours behind Greenwich Mean Time) and at Antiguan latitude, night was falling at 6:30 p.m. Before we started into our night shifts, Tori and I decided to have a little snuggle, and we had a good chat about our relationship. Over the course of the row, we had spoken about our future, and I knew we both intended to grow old together, but Tori told me she was worried that over the next year or so when she was back in Canada studying, we might grow apart and I might meet somebody else. I told her that I had these worries about her as well. After a good chat, I felt more at ease that we would make it work. I really do believe that Pup is my soulmate and that we were made for each other. We rowed hard during the night and made 83 kilometres (45 nautical miles) for the day. Considering the way things were looking that morning, I thought this a heroic effort. Our GPS now only showed two digits – less than 100 nautical miles (182.5 kilometres) to go!

I dreamt of the simple pleasures Antigua had in store for us. A real shower, a toilet that didn't move – and that flushed – a real bed, fruit, crisps, toast, a nice cup of tea, a beer. Actually, many beers. And then I started to think about my family and our friends Daragh Brehon and Miriam Walsh. I could hardly wait to see them all. I don't think I have ever looked forward to anything as much. One of the things I learned from the row was to enjoy life's simple pleasures, many of which I had been taking for granted.

All this talk of hugging our loved ones led us to a stark realization – we both stank. We decided to wash our shorts and T-shirts so that our families and friends would not pass out when we hugged them. We had no soap left so we used our coconut body wash. At least we would smell good. We had to wear the old, crusty shorts for the last few night shifts one last dose of pain. I think my threshold for pain had gone through the roof, so I wasn't that fussed. By morning on Wednesday, February 22, we had 75 kilometres (just over 40 nautical miles) to go. We would soon see Antigua. The promised land awaited.

Tori ....

I was giddy with excitement as we approached land. We had not yet spotted it nor smelt it, but it was close; we had just seen another shark following the boat and there were flocks of birds in view. We had a nice following wind and swell, so if we continued our normal rowing regime, we would probably reach our destination, English Harbour in Antigua, just after midnight. But it would be such a shame for our families to miss our coming in in daylight. I had been looking forward to the moment for over 80 days, and I really wanted to take it in. I wanted to see my mom crying as I came over the horizon and make eye contact with my dad, my brother and our dear friends.

We decided we would delay arriving until daylight the next day, Thursday, February 23, and we stopped for a few hours. We lunched and had a shower. We were so smelly I could not smell myself any more. I shaved my legs and armpits with one of our two rusty disposable razors, which were months old. We tidied the boat, scrubbed down the stains from the garbage bags and sprayed the cabin with oils to mask the smell of mould. I lay on the deck to top up my tan a little. After about 15 minutes of this we played cards, then tanned some more, played cards again . . . this was friggin' torture! For 84 days I had waited for the time when I could chill out and now that I finally had it I did not know what to do with myself. It was ironic, but all I wanted to do was row, when I had spent 84 days wanting to do anything but!

DAY 85, LAND!

When Paul spotted land, it was a surreal experience. It looked like a small pillow of clouds on the horizon, like a pillow sitting on the ocean. It was a very simple scene but so beautiful because I really felt I deserved it. When I finished my shift, I sat down, then lay on my back looking up to the clear blue sky, and all of a sudden I didn't want this experience to end. I felt we could keep going forever. As I cast my mind back over the last three months, I realized that through all the ups and downs I had fallen in love with something – the simple way of life out here. At this point it felt like second nature; when I was back on dry land I would be a fish out of water. What a great quality of life we had had: the most amazing skies, no pollution, no complications, no materialism. There was something very therapeutic about water. Even watching the wave patterns was like meditation.

We started into our final night shifts, and we were treated to a spectacular night sky. The entire galaxy seemed to be on display: nature giving us our final reward. All the pain and heartache of the last few months faded away as I found myself listening to Coldplay and giggling with excitement and happiness and a million other positive emotions while looking over my shoulder at the lights of Antigua and Guadeloupe.

At first we could only see the glare of the islands, as they were still slightly over the horizon. Then, as we got closer, we could see the individual lights on Antigua. Each time I woke up to do another night shift, Antigua looked so much closer. I was skipping out of the cabin for night shifts for the first time on the row. Now the lights covered the entire horizon. What a powerful feeling. Through the night, Paul and I reflected on the past three months. Maybe it was easy to say it now but I definitely thought it had been worth it – all the pain, sweat, blood and many tears. And now we were on the verge of completing our mammoth task!

Paul ··

For as long as I live, I will never forget that feeling when we saw land for the first time. Tori was rowing and I was standing in front of her, just outside the main cabin. My eyes suddenly opened wide, nearly peeling open my entire face. "Land! Tori! Land! There's land!" I pointed to the port side. "Do you swear on our relationship?" she asked. "Get up, look! It's land." We both stood gazing out at a tiny part of the world we had been dreaming of for three months. All we could see was the faded outline of the island still some 50-odd kilometres (25 nautical miles) away. We had made it! Tori resumed rowing, and I just stood there with a big stupid smile on my face. It was one of those special moments in life that we all sometimes have, one we knew we would remember forever.

That night was a special one, and I rowed with not a care in the world. The conditions were good and we reckoned we would make

Antigua by around 7 a.m. I reflected on all the good and bad times we had been through over the previous 85 days. I felt so proud of what we were about to achieve. We had worked like dogs to reach this point, and we would make Antigua. I thought about this as I looked over my right shoulder. I could see Antigua and the lights of Guadeloupe farther away again. We had fought hard to make sure we did not get blown there. It was a real achievement. The lights of Antigua seemed larger and clearer as we approached. I didn't want this night to end.

Over the course of the row, on clear nights we could see a constellation of stars in the shape of a question mark; I believe this is the Plough. On this last night, we were treated to an absolutely spectacular night sky. But now there was something different, and I don't know why. Now our question mark was upside down.

Tori ···

We stopped for breakfast at 4:45 a.m. Only 10 kilometres (5 nautical miles) to go. The island seemed huge. We had our navigation spot on; a slight northeast wind and the swell were pushing us exactly where we needed to go. We were both very proud of this. We cooked up our last "hot cereal with sultanas," brushed our teeth, washed our faces and chatted about how amazing it was to be on the verge of completing something unique.

There is a deep sense of pride when you know you have accomplished something huge on your own – with your own hands. There would be no bells or whistles when we came back to Ireland – maybe 15 minutes of fame, if we were lucky. I did not row this ocean as a publicity stunt, but for the quiet confidence I would carry around with me for the rest of my life. I would know in my heart I was an ocean rower.

At 6 a.m. we put in the second pair of oars and approached Antigua rowing together. On the horizon, dawn was just starting to break, the most beautiful rays of orange, red and yellow. The sun seemed so confident as it slowly rose into the sky. The day was calm and so was I; inside I knew I was ready for this. We had never rowed so fast together. Over my shoulder I kept looking at the brown mass of land. As the sun hit it, it was like someone was painting the scenery, dabbing in amazing shades of green on the cliffs. This must have been what it was like when Christopher Columbus first saw the other side of the world. The colours were stronger than I expected, but we hadn't seen such diversity in nearly three months. We spent the next hour or so just laughing. Wow! What had we done? It is very hard to put words to this feeling.

Paul

The GPS said less than a nautical mile (2 kilometres) to go. "Oh shit!" One of the buttons on my oar had broken. The button was the circular piece of plastic that stops the oar sliding out of the gate, which holds it in place. Tori threw me a screwdriver and I did some running repairs. Then my seat came off the rails along which it slides. I forced it back into place. "Come on. Come on! Just stay in place till we cross the finish line!" We had looked forward to this moment for so long, I wanted us both to be able to row across the finish line. Luckily everything held together. We had been told by the organizers that a RIB (rigid inflatable boat) would meet us and here it was. It stayed alongside us to officially record our crossing time. I studied the GPS as it counted down the last few hundred metres to zero. A foghorn blasted out as we triumphantly crossed the finish line. We hugged each other, ecstatic. Another moment I didn't want to end. We had another 3.7 kilometres (2 nautical miles) to go before we reached Nelson's Dockyard. I couldn't wait to see my family. I had never felt such emotion in all my life – it was magnificent!

Tori

I could hear the voice of my mother but could not see anyone. I felt a choke in the back of my throat as I fought overwhelming emotion. I had never felt such a feeling of having accomplished something. As we rowed into the bay behind the RIB, to our left I saw another small boat with four people waving flags frantically. I looked to my right as we passed cliffs and saw my dad. He was waving our Canadian flag so hard I thought he might fall off the cliff. I knew my parents and brother would do anything for me, but to actually see them here in person meant more to me than words could express. I spied my brother, Clayton, and our dear friends Daragh and Miriam. I was particularly proud to share this experience with Dar and Mir, as they must have felt they had rowed this ocean with us. They had been the only ones to stand next to us from day 1; they witnessed the struggle from beginning to end.

I tried to keep in time with Paul as we approached the boatyard. Boats honked their foghorns and there was even a Canadian couple waving a flag next to us. I felt I had made my country proud; this was a once-in-a-lifetime experience. What really got me was when I saw my dad running down the cliff with his uncoordinated stride. We slowed down to make sure he made it in time. We confidently turned the boat around to show off our rowing skills to all who had never seen us row and then we tied up. "Ladies first," Paul said, and I got off the boat. He's not usually so polite – he just wanted to see if I was going to fall over! One leg onto terra firma. The texture felt so foreign. Another leg, oops! It was like my brain and my feet were not connected. I felt like a baby trying to walk again as I wobbled sideways. As I looked up, I saw Mom. Like a mother bear she fought through the crowd and scooped up her young cub. The entire boatyard seemed to erupt in tears. I think I have never embraced my mother so much. Dad and Clay joined the hug, exposing their softness to the world. I hugged my family as though I had not seen them in decades. I didn't want to ever let them go. I hoped I would be able to show my love to them one day as they had demonstrated theirs to me that day.

Paul ⋯⋯⋯⋯⋯⋯⋯⋯⋯⋯⋯⋯⋯⋯⋯⋯⋯⋯⋯⋯⋯⋯⋯⋯⋯⋯⋯⋯⋯⋯⋯⋯⋯⋯⋯⋯⋯

As we approached the harbour, I could see my parents, my sister, my Aunt Irene and Tori's mom all waving their flags frantically in the RIB. My heart began to race; I was deliriously happy and couldn't wait to embrace them. Yet I didn't want this moment to end. I shed a tear at the sight of my family. I don't think I had ever experienced such emotion.

When we reached the quayside, I looked down to plant my right foot on dry land and it seemed like such an alien action. I wobbled like a dazed boxer on the ropes and embraced Mam with the most heartfelt embrace I had ever given her. Her first words to me? "Don't ever do this again, please." Then my dad and my sister, Audrey, came in to the hug. After all we had been through, we were united again in a big family hug, and boy did it feel good.

My Aunt Irene joined in. I was really honoured that she was there to share this with us. Irene, who lives in Chicago, had lost her husband, Bob, while we were at sea, and although he had been ill for quite a long time, it must had been heartbreaking for her. I was so happy she had decided to come down to Antigua.

It was magic. To have my family and Daragh and Miriam there meant more to me than I would ever be able to express. It was almost like a dream. Except we were living the dream!

CHAPTER 30
Life after the Row

Tori ⸱⸱⸱

Naturally, after hugging my family and friends, I looked for any sign of food. Steph Temperton from the *Making Waves* team came flying down to the boatyard with a hot bag of fresh croissants and apple turnovers. As I snatched them out of her hand, she gave me a sympathetic smile and I knew she understood; she had been here for about a week. I took no notice as the crowd watched me wolf down the turnover. This was so like the first time my mom gave me junk food as a child. I was in ecstasy! Now I could be part of society again and talk to all those who had come to support us.

We headed up to a house our parents had rented for everybody. What a bizarre feeling walking up the stairs and into the rooms! I could not comprehend how much space there was – the bloody couch was bigger than our boat! The first thing I wanted to do was have a shower, as the two sets of parents prepared the best meal of all time – a proper Irish breakfast imported to Antigua. I stood in the shower, warm water beating down over my head, the salt running off my body. I was in an outside shower and the smell of plants and greenery was heaven. A small beetle ran across the floor. I was fascinated by it, as I had not seen any such creatures for the last three months. The simple things seemed to be really getting me. As the smell of the shampoo reached my nose I started to feel civilized again; I was a real person, maybe even a lady.

I started to spin a little as my legs wanted to give way; I had not stood for as long as this for the entire trip. I left the shower to sit on the toilet, naked as the day I was born. "Mom! Mom!" I cried. She came to my rescue. I had been so looking forward to sitting on a toilet that did not move; now I was still moving but the toilet was not moving with me. I braced myself as I swayed back and forth, with Mom holding me until it passed. She helped me stand up and put my bathing suit on as though I were two years old again. I am sure she was loving the opportunity to mother me again.

I sat down to breakfast. The smell of a sausage brought a tear to my eye. As I bit into a slice of wholemeal bread I felt a sense of relief – there was fibre in here; I would shit again. I know it seems a small thing but the prospect of a proper bowel movement cheered me. We ate and ate. It seemed to go on for at least two hours. Daragh was on toast duty and it just kept coming. As I sat and devoured my lunch, I stopped and realized everyone was just looking at us as though we were going to disappear. And it dawned on me that I was actually in someone else's company other than Paul's. How bizarre!

All day I kept looking at my mom and dad, Clay, Dar and Mir and just wanted to hug them. I never wanted this time to end. I had rowed an ocean and now my family were together around me. This was the best thing I could have, the best thing I would ever do, my greatest accomplishment.

Paul

Later that evening, we sat on the bed and dialled Eamonn Kavanagh's number. When he answered, Tori and I proudly announced that we had made it to Antigua. Eamonn was delighted and congratulated us. We told him that after we crossed the finish line, the RIB, which was the local search and rescue boat, had come out to clock our official time and asked us if we wanted a tow to the marina. "Tell me youse didn't take a tow," said Eamonn after a pause. We said we didn't: it was important for us to row the entire way across, no tows, no assistance, just us. "*Christina* doesn't like to be towed," we replied. "Thank God you didn't take the tow, because if you did, Peter wouldn't have regarded you as rowing across the Atlantic," said Eamonn.

The next day Tori's brother, Clayton, woke us at 5 a.m. to say some radio show was looking for us: the Gerry Ryan Show on RTÉ Radio 2 FM. As I started to get out of the bed the ceiling started moving, then the room was a bit wobbly and my legs went from underneath me. I fell on the floor. Tori chuckled. When we finished the interview, we went back to bed. We hadn't been there that long anyway. God, it felt great to sleep in a real bed again.

So there it was; we had just rowed across the Atlantic Ocean. It didn't sink in straightaway. Even now as I write this several months later, I don't think it has fully hit me. I don't think about it that often, but every now and then somebody will say something or I'll come across a picture that gets my mind going and I will stop and think to myself, "Hey, I rowed an ocean. Wow!"

The simple pleasures in Antigua were all that we had hoped for. All those things I dreamt of – seeing and spending time with my family and friends again, having a shower, using a toilet that doesn't try to throw me off, toast, fresh fruit, a beer . . .

For me, the row was a hugely humbling experience. It made me appreciate how lucky I am in life and how fortunate I've been. It also made me realize how much my family mean to me. I have been asked many times since I've been back if I get sick of talking about it, but I was always flattered to think that people were interested in something Tori and I did. I could not honestly say that it changed me in any spiritual way or that I discovered a deep, meaningful love of God or anything like that, but the row definitely put a lot of things into perspective for me. I had three months to think about my life and, more important, what I wanted to do. That aspect of the row was unique: to have so much time to think about my life, what I had done in the past and where I wanted to go in the future. We're all so busy these days that I don't think most of us ever get time to stop, take a breath and just have some time for ourselves.

One thing I will say, and I don't think it is being arrogant, but I genuinely believe that if I really want to do something in life and work hard toward achieving it, then I can do it. Nothing can stop me if I truly want it.

Shortly after we returned to Ireland, I was getting my car washed. I was sitting in the car reading the newspaper as the guy outside worked away. He started singing to himself, his voice muffled by the splash of the power hose, and all of a sudden I was back out on the ocean again, in the cabin listening to one of Tori's concerts. Every now and then there is a moment like this that takes me back to our Atlantic adventure. Yes, I miss it – not necessarily the pain and all the suffering we went through, but the good times: the adventure, the journey into the un-known, the simple pleasures of the ocean, having a dip to cool down on a warm day, sitting with the woman I love watching the sun go down as we chat aimlessly about life. I miss how simple and uncomplicated our lives were for those few precious months. Granted, it was dangerous at times, but I think now I can appreciate what people mean when they talk about how special the ocean is. It really is magical out there, and something that just has to be experienced to be truly understood.

Tori and I went to England shortly after the row to attend an awards night for all the rowers from the 2005/2006 race. It was great to meet up with everybody again and swap war stories. One of the other rowers told us a tale of pirates picking up the crew of one of the boats that capsized. It was strange to hear this story because I remember one night during the row we saw navigation lights for two ships virtually on top of each other, which was very, very strange. It was the middle of the night and we wondered why two boats would be so close to each other. To us it appeared that they were more or less side by side. We wondered if one of the ships could be a pirate one. Although we doubted it, we turned off our navigation light to avoid being spotted. Who knows what was going on that night? In hindsight, maybe what seemed like paranoia may have been good sense!

Would I do it all again? Definitely! Will I do it again? Who knows? Probably not, as I couldn't afford to – we owe too much money from this row, and I think my parents would kill me if I told them I wanted to do another ocean.

One way in which I have changed forever is that I can no longer go to sleep lying on my back. While we were out on the ocean, the only way I could fall asleep when things were really wild and rough was to lie on my stomach, spread my legs out and brace my feet off each side of the cabin so as to stop myself getting thrown around. Although the legs don't quite form the V they did on the boat, to this day, months after the row, I have yet to fall asleep on my back. I guess life will never be the same again.

ATLANTIC ROWING RACE 2005/2006
Overall Race Rankings

Rank Order	Boat No.	Boat Name	Team Names
1st	8	C2	Chris Andrews and Clint Evans 51 days 2 hours 10 minutes
2nd	5	Atlantic 4	George Simpson, David Martin, Glynn Coupland and Neil Wrightwick 49 days 14 hrs 21 mins (Used 60 litres of water ballast; dropped one place)
3rd	24	All Relative	Justin Adkin, Martin Adkin, Robert Adkin and James Green 39 days 3 hrs 32 mins (Used 120 litres of water ballast; dropped two places)
4th	30	Spirit of EDF Energy	Ben Fogle and James Cracknell 49 days 19 hrs 8 mins (Used 60 litres of water ballast; dropped one place)
5th	20	Bout de vie	Frank Bruno and Dominique Benassi 54 days 3 hrs 31 mins
6th	14	Atlantic Prince	Dan Darley and Richard Dewire 58 days 12 hrs 16 mins
7th	27	Team Scandlines	Christian Petersen and Soren Sprogoe 59 days 9 hrs 6 mins
8th	33	Row 4 Cancer	Liz O'Keeffe and Richard Mayon-White 60 days 18 hrs 56 mins
9th	10	Mayabrit	Andrew Barnett and Juan Carlos Sagastume Bendana 64 days 13 hrs 17 mins
10th	16	Gurkha Spirit	Al Howard and Nick Rowe 66 days 13 hrs 16 mins
11th	17	Mission Atlantic	Paula Evemy, Kathy Tracey, Lois Rawlins-Duquemin and Sarah Day 67 days 7 hrs 20 mins
12th	18	Mark 3	Rob Eustace and Peter Williams 68 days 1 hr 3 mins
13th	3	Christina	Paul Gleeson and Tori Holmes 84 days 23 hrs 12 mins (Used 10 litres of water ballast; 7-hour time penalty)

The following seven teams were disqualified for breach of race rules and received no official race ranking. They appear below in the order that they finished. Although disqualified from the race, these teams are fully credited with rowing across the Atlantic.

Boat No.	Boat Name	Team Names
22	Atlantic Warrior	Tom Bright and Charles Bairsto
4	Row 4 Life	Charlie Woodward-Fisher and Philip Harris
88	Charmed Life	Andrew Morris and Mick Dawson
5	Pacific Pete	Chris Martin
7	Making Waves	Rebecca Thorpe and Stephanie Temperton
11	Rowgirls.com	Jo Davies, Sally Kettle, Claire Mills and Sue McMillan
15	Sedna Solo	Roz Savage

The following teams were rescued on the ocean and forced to retire from the race:

Boat No.	Boat Name	Team Names
1	Digicel Atlantic Challenge	Gearóid Towey and Ciaran Lewis
25	Team Sun Latte	Tara Remington and Iain Rudkin
12	American Fire	Sarah Kessans and Emily Kohl
23	Moveahead	Bobby Prentice and Colin Briggs
9	Spirit of Cornwall	Chris Barrett and Bob Warren
2	Serenity Now	Duncan Pearson and Gareth Pearson

OTHER TITLES AVAILABLE FROM RMB

Expedition to the Edge

Stories of Worldwide Adventure

Lynn Martel

$22.95 Softcover ISBN 978-1897522097

Lynn Martel has assembled 59 compelling and enter-taining stories that uniquely capture the exploits, hard-ships, fears and personal insights of a virtual who's who of contemporary adventurers as they explore remote landscapes from the Rockies to Pakistan to Antarctica.

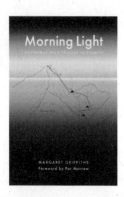

Morning Light

Triumph at Sea & Tragedy on Everest

Margaret Griffiths | Foreword by Pat Morrow

$29.95 Hardcover ISBN 978-1897522080

Written from taped accounts, diaries, letters and reports, Morning Light: Triumph at Sea & Tragedy on Everest is a poignant saga of adventure and high emotion that celebrates the human spirit and its need to explore.

Adventurous Dreams, Adventurous Lives

Edited by Jason Schoonover | Foreword by Meave Leakey

$29.95 Softcover ISBN 978-1894765916

120 outstanding individuals recall the indelible mo-ment in their youth when the dream that launched their remarkable lives was born. As they recount the turning points to fulfilling those dreams - how they often over-came enormous physical, emotional or other obstacles - we learn how extraordinarily inspirational their lives are.